SteamDrunks

101 Steampunk Cocktails and Mixed Drinks

Chris-Rachael Oseland

To my sister from another mister, Anne.

Here's to the next 20 years.

Table of Contents

STEAMPUNK COCKTAIL BASICS

Be honest. You bought this book because you thought it was going to be an endless parade of gin and absinthe, maybe with a little rum thrown in for people who cosplay Airship Sky Pirates. You'll find those drinks near the end. Compared to what most people were really drinking in the 19th century, those familiar concoctions are downright boring.

First, I'm taking you on an adventure through improbable uses of household staples. You'll find punch recipes you could confuse for farmer's cheese, tea recipes that will knock you out rather than wake you up, and downright chewable eggy cream curdles. The Victorian era was a different world, with different ideas about hygiene, potency, and cirrhosis.

Along the way, you'll also find some shockingly tasty 19th century recipes using all natural ingredients you already have at home.

In the spirit of authenticity, you won't find any recipes using artificial flavors or chemical substitutes in here. Don't get me wrong. The pinnacle of modernity can be summed up by chocolate pie flavored vodka served in a candy cane shooter glass and topped with cherry flavored nondairy alcoholic whipped cream, none of which include any ingredients found outside a chemistry set. Imagine everything necessary to make that cheap, tasty drink possible. It's awe inspiring. We live in the future.

Sometimes, though, it's fun to visit the past. Part of Steampunk's allure is pulling back the veil of time and enjoying a simpler world full of optimism, enthusiasm, and objects real people can make with their own hands. Or, in the case of these recipes, drinks real people can mix in their own kitchens. They're more labor intensive than simply throwing three types of vodka in a martini glass and calling it a cocktail, but the genuine flavors of the 19th century are worth it.

Stocking Your Steampunk Bar

Vodka cocktails are a relatively recent invention. Your authentic 19th century Steampunk alcohols of choice are:

Brandy
Whiskey
Rum
Gin
Vermouth
Hard Cider
Red Wine
Champagne

Forget your modern mixers. For Steampunk drinks, you'll need:

Milk
Cream
Eggs
Sugar
Tea
Lemons
Limes
Oranges
Cinnamon Sticks
Fresh nutmeg and a small grater
Bitters

You can now make 3/4 of the cocktails in this book. Throw in some flour, butter and baking powder and you can also make a cake.

MILK DRINKS

The Victorians liked nothing better than a drink they could chew. Below, my fine ladies and gentlemen, you will find a plethora of recipes where curdling is the desired effect. Let these drinks sit out too long and a few of them are halfway to becoming alcoholic cheese.

Thank goodness for Steampunk.

If we were authentic Victorian recreationists, our ladies wouldn't proudly wear their undergarments on the outside of their clothes and every gear we owned would actually have a function. Pshaw, I say. If we can send lightning thieves up in airships by golly we can create a thick, creamy beverage that can't be confused for spoiled paneer.

While I don't like to chew my drinks, I do like to come as close as possible to recreating an authentic flavor of the time. That's why, for the following recipes, I lean heavily towards the two milk substitutes which would've been available in 19th century kitchens - almond milk and coconut milk.

Creating almond milk involved a labor intensive process favored by patriotic sorts who didn't want to muck about with all those foreign ingredients. It's thin, brown, and naturally low fat with a faintly nutty but mostly neutral flavor that blends into the background of your drink.

5

Coconut milk, on the other hand, will provide you a richer, creamier texture more reminiscent of actual dairy without the pesky curdling, but at the cost of adding a notable flavor influenced by the furthest reaches of the British Empire. In many cases, you're best off mixing the two.

You can always pick up store bought milk substitute beverages, but the first ingredient in most of those is sugar or high fructose corn syrup. They're wonderful inventions, but speaking from experience, they'll give you a radically different flavor from that enjoyed by the Victorians.

In the spirit of authenticity, I offer you a recipe for almond milk. It's terrible on cereal and absolute rubbish for whitening your tea, but it makes a surprisingly good mixed drink.

Victorian Almond Milk

4 cups Almonds
1 cup roughly chopped Dates
12-16 cups Water
Cheesecloth
Large stock pot
Colander

Buy the cheapest unsalted, raw almonds and dates you can find in bulk. They don't need to be pretty. Dump the almonds into your food processor and grind those nuts like the souls of your indentured staff. When you have a coarse meal, throw in the dates. These provide an authentic period sweetness. If you're feeling lazy you can add half a cup of sugar instead. Whatever you do, don't add any honey or molasses. If you do, congratulations, you're halfway towards making a semi-palatable gluten free pie crust. You want powdery almonds, not a sticky mess.

Once you've ground your almonds and dates down to the texture of coarse whole grain flour, it's time to add the water. Fill your food processor with as much water as it can handle and pulse a few more times until everything is nicely blended.

Now it's time for a nice game of Russian nesting dolls. Line a colander with your cheesecloth. Put the cheesecloth lined colander into your stock pot. Now carefully pour the contents of your food processor into the cheesecloth lined colander and let it slowly drain into the stockpot.

You should now have a heavy, damp mass of almonds in the colander and a thin gray-brown fluid in the stockpot. Congratulations on making almond milk! I tend to go for 3 pressings in order to leach all the tasty goodness out of the almonds.

Squeeze the cheesecloth like you're strangling a poacher. When it's dry and lifeless, dump the almonds back into your food processor, refill it with water, and pulse again until you have a second batch of almond slurry. Once more, carefully strain it into the cheesecloth lined colander. Repeat the process one last time as though you're ekeing the last essence from a gelfling's soul.

If you want to concentrate the flavor of your almond milk you can now put it on a boil and reduce it by up to 1/3.

Since you have a honking mass of almond flour left over, you can always add some oats, butter, cinnamon and honey in order to make a tasty fruit crumble topping. Ignore advice that says the leftover grounds from almond milk make a good body scrub. Those lying bastards just want to see how many people will spackle their armpits together.

Cognac Milk

1 shot Cognac
1 shot Dark Creme de Cacao
1 shot Whole Cream
Fresh ground Nutmeg

Unlike most milk drinks, this hearty winter cocktail was actually meant to be served cold. If your evening is destined to involve a generous amount of drinking, indulge in the whole cream. Your battered, drunken body will appreciate the fat and calories while your mind appreciates the spirits.

Pour your Cognac, Creme de Cacao and whole cream into a cocktail shaker full of ice. Pummel the shaker so roughly people think you're trying to make butter. Gently pour the frothy mix into a martini glass and top it with a dusting of fresh ground nutmeg. If you ignore the disturbing similarity to Santorum, you'll find it a refreshing and filling drink.

Alexander

1 shot Gin
1 shot Light Creme de Cacao
1 shot Whole Cream
Dash Bitters

Unlike Cognac Milk, the Alexander was meant to be enjoyed at room temperature. Add all of your ingredients to a lowball glass and stir vigorously. You can dress it up by garnishing it with a mint leaf, or perhaps a cube of cheese, but whatever you do, don't add a slice of fruit.

Cautious modern drinkers may want to throw out the bitters in favor of a cup full of ice. Smart modern drinkers will ignore the gin's angry taunts and go make some Cognac Milk instead.

Whiskey Milk

1/2 cup Whole Milk
1 shot Whiskey
1/2 shot Sugar
Fresh grated Cinnamon or Nutmeg

Readers may notice a theme here. Remember, the 19th century was a time when anything liquid was probably full of deadly bacteria. Both water and milk were so unsafe children often went from the breast straight to the pint.

This calcium-rich recipe dangerously includes more milk than alcohol. Serve it either to bare knuckle boxers who live for danger or your least favorite son after he loses three fingers at the textile mill. Either way, buy some insurance first.

Originally, this would've been made from room temperature ingredients. Modern drinkers are advised to pour the whiskey and sugar in a highball glass and stir them together until the sugar is mostly melted. Add some nice pasteurized, chilled whole milk, then decadently top off the glass with ice, you weak dandy.

Ugandan Ginger Tea

1 cup Milk
1 tsp Black Tea Leaves
1 tbsp Sugar
1/4 tsp fresh grated raw Ginger (or a small dash of tinned ginger paste)
4 shots Rum

Before introducing you to the horrors of Victorian milk punches, let's ease you in with a heartily drinkable beverage not destined to curdle for your guest's amusement.

Bring the milk to a simmer. Add the tea leaves and freshly grated ginger. Reduce the heat and allow the flavors to mingle for at least 10 minutes. (Ahem. Modern drinkers may prefer a weaker tea simmered for under 3 minutes. It all depends on how much hair you want on your chest.)

Strain out the tea leaves. Add the sugar and rum to the hot milk mixture and whisk everything until it's as frothy as your grandmother's spittle. Pour the result into four large teacups and serve with ginger biscuits.

Peach Milk Punch

2 cups Whole Milk
2 cups Peach Brandy
1 cup Weak Ale
1 cup Sugar
1 cup Crushed Violet Leaves

This would've been considered a respectable afternoon punch with one serving for 8 people. A hostess need only mix everything but 1/2 cup of violet leaves together the morning before the party then let the entire mix stew at room temperature. That's right. Day old, unpasteurized, room temperature milk is the base of this cocktail. When you laugh at the face of death every morning at breakfast, there's no reason not to conquer the world before tea.

Before her guests arrived, an elegant hostess could garnish the punch by sprinkling her remaining 1/2 cup of reserved violet leaves on top. If she wanted a little fashionable curdling, she could always add the juice of four oranges to give the drink a little chunkiness going down.

Yes, Victorian drinks had a texture and aroma you can't find in any modern bars.

Let's give this a nice Steampunk revision.

2 cups Peach Brandy
1 cup Hard Cider
1 cup Coconut Milk
1 cup Almond Milk
1/4 cup Sugar
Juice of 2 Oranges

Mix everything together in a fetching punchbowl. Leave it in the fridge for a minimum of four hours so the flavors can get to know one another a little better. If you're feeling daring, go ahead and add in a cinnamon stick.

For a slightly more authentic flavor, omit the oranges, double the sugar, and use whole milk. Don't forget the cider, though. It may sound about as appealing as an octopus crawling up your leg, but much like quality hentai, this drink is surprisingly better than anyone is willing to admit.

Fine Milk Punch

1/2 gallon Whole Milk
1/2 gallon Water
1/2 gallon Brandy or Rum
10 large Lemons
2 cups Sugar
2 tbsp grated Nutmeg

Welcome to the wonderful world of truly exotic period drinks. Just look at that recipe. Half a gallon of milk and the juice of 10 lemons. The instructions are distressingly similar to making cheese, as is the end result. Trust me when I say you've never made anything like it. A quality punch like this takes two days to really set. Get ready for some kitchen adventures.

Carefully zest the rind off all 10 lemons. This is a good time to buy organic in order to avoid eating a heaping mouth full of pesticides. If you don't own a zester, you can use a potato peeler, but be extra careful to only use the outermost yellow skin, not the bitter white interior.

Steep the lemon zest in the brandy or rum for 24 hours. Meanwhile, mix your lemon juice, sugar, nutmeg, and milk. Let that sexy pot sit for 24 hours as well.

Remember, refrigeration is only for feeble foreigners!

The next day, add your water to your room temperature milk mix and bring it to a boil. Add the rum or brandy. Let everything simmer together for ten minutes then let it cool.

Once cool, strain the concoction through cheesecloth. Serve the liquidy part and, in the spirit of authenticity, use the remaining solids as a garnish around the bowl.

Now, let's say you're not in the mood to make dubiously alcoholic cheese. A modern Steampunk variation would substitute the whole milk for coconut milk while cutting the quantity of sugar and water in half. Mix all the ingredients together with a mere half hour for the flavors to flirt before serving the concoction on ice. This iteration of the drink lacks the spirited danger of potential listeria poisoning, so instead of Fine Milk Punch you might have to rename it Weak, Adequate Colonial Milk Punch.

Strong Colonial Milk Punch

1 gallon Rum or Brandy
1/2 gallon Milk
8 Seville Oranges
8 large Lemons
4 Egg Shells and Whites
6 cups Sugar
12 cups Water

Finely zest (or very carefully peel then dice) the skin of your lemons and oranges. Add the zest to the rum or brandy then go find something else to amuse yourself with for a day. Good drinks take patience.

When you return, make a nice simple syrup by bringing the water to a boil and adding the sugar. Stir until the sugar melts, then let it boil until the concoction is reduced by at least 2 cups. Meanwhile, beat the egg whites into a nice froth and crumble the shells. Add those to your simple syrup and keep boiling until a scum rises to the top.

Once you have a nice scummy solution, skim it then strain it through cheesecloth until your liquid is perfectly clear. Clean your pot (or get a new one, you wastrel) and fill it with your nicely strained sugar solution and the strained juice of all your fruit. Make sure there are no seeds or pulp in the mix.

Strain the fruit zest from your brandy or rum. Add the strained alcohol to the nicely skimmed sugar solution. Let it cool to lukewarm, then add your whole milk. Mix it all together. If you have a cask lying around, pour everything inside and bung it up. If you don't, put a lid on your pot and put it in a cool, dark place.

Your Strong Colonial Punch is allegedly drinkable in six weeks, though considered far better if left to sit for a full six months. While you wait, feel free to amuse yourself reading about 19th century food poisoning deaths.

Milk Punch Another Way

8 cups Water
6 cups Brandy
4 cups Whole Milk
10 large Lemons
4 cups Sugar
*2 cups Ratafia (or your choice of strong herb
flavored liquor)*

You should detect a pattern by now. Go on, rip the
rind off those lemons. The brandy is waiting for a
sexy lemon infusion. Once the peels have a day or
more to soak, bring your milk to a boil. Add the
water, brandy, juice of the 10 lemons, and sugar. Stir
well until everything seems perfectly blended. Let the
mix cool then strain it through an old flannel shirt.
Cheesecloth is for those lazy bastards who inherited
their money. If this shirt was good enough for your
grandfather, it's good enough for your cocktail. Once
strained, add the Ratafia and mix well.

You now have two things. Serve the liquid to people.
Give the curds to your hogs. If you don't have any
hogs, give the curds to your servants.

Modern Steampunks will find the bitter herb liquor
provides a very nice counterpoint to strong lemon
flavor. If you're feeling fancy, go ahead and make a
lemon infused simple syrup by boiling the water,
lemon, and sugar together until the sugar is melted

and the liquid is clear. Meanwhile, soak the lemon peels in the brandy. This can be done up to 2 days in advance. When you're ready to serve the punch, mix your simple syrup, strained brandy, and bitter herb liquor with two pints of almond milk.

The modern variation can be served either warm in tea cups or over ice in lowball glasses, depending on the weather.

Poor Milk Punch

4 cups Old Milk, not yet fully turned
2 cups Brandy
6 Lemons or Oranges
1 cup Sugar

Once more, zest your oranges or lemons. This time, who needs the pesky, potentially hygienic step of boiling? Be bold! Be daring! Juice that citrus and throw it in a pot with your old milk, brandy, juice, rind, and sugar. Let the scary mix sit at room temperature for two days. When you've almost forgotten what you left lurking in the pantry, it's time to pour the entire mix into a jelly bag or flannel shirt and position it over a large pot. Squeeze, strain, and separate the liquids from the solids.

Any liquids that drip through are allegedly deemed potable. The alcohol content is probably high enough to make you forget the utter misery of a life where straining milk through flannel shirts equals a fun Saturday night. In modern times, this recipe is recommended for homeless people who live in a dumpster near a Whole Foods or minimum security prison inmates.

If, however, you find yourself spontaneously throwing a room party at a Steampunk convention and need a fast, inexpensive Victorian themed drink to sauce up the masses, you could always try the following variation.

4 cups Almond Milk
2 cups cheap Brandy
6 cups Orange Juice
1 cup Sugar (or 50 stolen sugar packets)

Go ahead and buy pre-made almond milk from the grocery store. If you're making this version, you're in a hurry. Throw everything in a punchbowl, stir vigorously, and make pretentious drunken noises about your attention to authenticity. After all, despite what you're actually serving, you know how to make this drink from scratch. You were merely out of both flannel and time.

Norfolk Punch

4 gallons Rum
3 gallons Orange Juice
1/2 gallon Whole Milk
12 Egg Whites
6 gallons Water
6 pounds Sugar
12 Oranges
12 Lemons
4 Cinnamon Sticks

You know the drill. Zest or carefully peel the oranges and lemons. Let all that citrus peel steep in your rum for 24 hours. Meanwhile, juice the oranges and lemons and store the result in a separate container.

The next day, mix your egg whites until they're frothy and add them to the water. Bring that to a boil and mix in the sugar and cinnamon sticks. Keep stirring until the sugar melts. By now, you should have a little froth rising to the top. Skim off as much as you can.

Once you get bored with skimming scum, let your mixture cool to room temperature. You've now made cinnamon infused simple syrup!

Fish out the cinnamon sticks then add the rum, orange juice, and the juice of the 12 lemons. Stir well. Now add the milk. Pour your concoction into a tightly sealed container and leave it somewhere cool and dark for the next two months.

Two months later, strain the punch through four layers of cheesecloth or a flannel shirt. You can drink it down or now bottle the result in order to preserve the flavor of the Duke of Norfolk's slightly woolen flavored homestyle brew.

Windsor Rock Punch

4 cups Heavy Cream
2 cups of liquid from canned Maraschino Cherries
1 cup Kirsch
1 cup Clear Rum
1 cup Sugar
12 Eggs

Yes, this punch was indeed created to be served to the Windsor family. Ice cream was an expensive and impressive novelty in the 19th century. Today, it's a staple of timed cooking shows. Only you can judge the connection.

Bring the cream to a simmer. Whisk in the sugar and eggs. Don't bring it to a hard boil - for once, you don't want to risk cooking the eggs or curdling the milk. When your mix has simmered cheerfully for 10 minutes, put it in an ice cream maker.

When the ice cream is still a little runny, remove half of it from the mixer and add the Maraschino cherry liquid, kirsch and rum. Mix well. It should be a little slushy. Go ahead and finish freezing the rest of the ice cream until rock hard.

To serve, neatly fill a martini or round champagne glass 2/3 full of alcoholic slush then use a large melon baller to add a neat scoop of the plain ice cream to the middle. If it's good enough for the Windsor's, it's good enough for your guests.

Vanilla Bourbon Punch

4 cups Whole Milk
3 cups Bourbon
1 cup Water
1 cup Sugar
2 Vanilla Beans, seeds scraped and pods reserved
Fresh grated Nutmeg

After the curdling cocktails, this is almost disappointingly drinkable. It's amazing they didn't want to add a pineapple just to muddle up the flavors and turn things nice and chunky.

In addition to being more tasty than interesting, this drink is also surprisingly easy to make. You don't even need old clothing or half a citrus tree.

Simply put the water, sugar, and vanilla beans (both seeds and pods) into a small saucepan. Bring the mix to a boil, put a lid on the pot, and remove it from the heat. After it steeps for at least 15 minutes, strain it.

Yes you are once more being seduced into making a simple syrup. Vanilla simple syrup is a wonderful addition to drinks, so feel free to triple the quantity you're making and save the excess in an airtight, room temperature container.

Once the vanilla simple sugar cools, throw it in your punch bowl. Add the milk and bourbon to the party and stir well. Top the whole mix with a light dusting of fresh grated nutmeg.

To serve, fill a lowball glass with ice and top it off with the disappointingly decent punch.

EGG DRINKS

Nothing makes for a quality party quite like a roaring case of salmonella.

It's tempting to look upon these drinks with an anthropological eye. Sugar was a preservative. Alcohol was both a preservative and an antiseptic. You needed lots of both to make dubious things like eggs and milk safe to drink.

Now, to give the Victorians credit, they didn't have issues with factory farm overcrowding or chickens being kept high on a cocktail of antibiotics, growth hormones, and the zombie brains of their fallen comrades. Plus, when you lived next to a river as dubiously crunchy as the Thames, you got into the habit of adding a bit of sweet, purifying alcohol to any ingestible liquids.

Being forced to drink water would've been just as terrifyingly gross to them as having raw chicken breasts rubbed on the inside of our nostrils to us. Burning out disease with the fire of booze worked on your uncle Timmy, the family ox, and by God it'll work on this bowl of eggs.

Brave Steampunks who indulge in these cocktails should spend a few extra dollars on pasteurized eggs. If they're not available at your local grocery, at least improve your odds with free range organic eggs.

Consumption might have been a sexy disease, but no one wrote poems about the seductive impact of salmonella on their beloved's body.

White House Egg Nog

1/2 gallon Whole Milk
8 Eggs
8 tbsp Sugar
8 wine glasses Brandy
3 wine glasses Rum

Unlike the often chunky milk punches, egg nogs were meant to be a smooth, creamy treat. I left the original "wine glass" measures to give you a bit of flexibility. In this context, glasses held about six ounces. While a couple glasses of this would put most of us under the table, the Victorians had livers as strong as the whalebone in their corsets. Modern drinkers might use a wineglass which could be mistaken for a shot. No one will tell.

Separate the egg whites from the yolks. Beat the yolks like they're a disobedient stablehand, then add the sugar so they know you still care.

Slowly add in the alcohols until the entire beating incident is a bit muddled. Meanwhile, off in a different bowl, whip some spine into those limp egg whites. When they've stiffened up, add the milk and about half the egg whites to the yolk mixture. Continue beating until the two cleave together for their own protection. Gently stir in the rest of the pre-beaten egg whites.

Let the drink sit in your fridge for at least half an hour so the flavors can come to terms with what just happened to them. Serve in small teacups if you used the period recipe or hearty mugs if scaled to modern tastes.

If you're too tired to engage in all that beating and whipping feel free to save time by resorting to a blender, you lazy degenerate.

Kentucky Egg Nog

24 Eggs
1/2 gallon Whole Milk
4 cups Cream
4 cups Brandy
8 cups Rum
4 cups Sugar
Freshly grated Nutmeg

As you can see, the White House was a demure place compared to the great state of Kentucky. This recipe was meant as light refreshment for 20 people before the serious drinking began.

Once more, separate your egg yolks from your whites. Beat the egg yolks (or dump them into a blender) until they're a thick yellow mass, then add in the sugar. Continue beating or blending until you have a dubiously thick yellow mass.

Dump the sugary egg blend into your punchbowl and add in the milk, cream, brandy and rum. Feel your arteries harden as you blend it all into a single creamy concoction.

Next, throw your egg whites into a bowl and abuse them with a hand mixer until they magically transform from a sticky liquid into stiff white peaks.

Artistically float the beaten egg whites on top of the egg nog.

Serve cool, but not iced, with a generous sprinkle of fresh nutmeg on top. If you suspect two glasses of this high octane egg nog will leave you with such little manual dexterity you're more likely to grate your own fingers than the nutmeg, go ahead and generously dust the top of the punch with nutmeg before adding the egg whites. No one will remember the difference tomorrow.

Orange Egg Nog

1/2 cup Cream
1/2 cup Whole Milk
1/2 cup Brandy
1/2 cup Rum
2 Eggs
2 tbsp Sugar
Juice of 2 Oranges
1 cup Pineapple or Apricot Juice

Nothing says class like a good room temperature curdle. The Victorians were delighted by drinks you could chew.

An authentic re-creation of this drink would involve throwing all the room temperature ingredients into a bowl, beating the mix to the best of your ability, letting it sit half a day, then serving it to a party of four. Anything less than a quarter cup of hard alcohol per person would be considered irredeemably stingy.

As for all that delicious dairy, the longer you take to sip, the more curdles in your glass.

The 19th century was an era of limited entertainment.

With a little modification, it's easy to turn this into a nicely alcoholic version of an Orange Julius. Try substituting whole fat coconut milk for the cream and period almond milk (see the chapter on Milk Drinks) for the whole milk.

Dump your milk substitutes and all the other ingredients into a blender and let the magic of electricity create a single smooth substance. Pour the result into ice filled lowball glasses. Take a sip. That's right. Ignore your shock when you realize you want more. Marvel that this is actually a great flavor combination.

You're welcome.

Egg Restorative

1 Egg
1/2 cup Whole Milk
1/4 cup Brandy
2 tsp Sugar
1/2 tsp Salt
Dash Bitters

This drink was presented as a medicinal beverage for soothing sore stomachs. Apparently, nothing says comfort like a salty, bitter raw egg.

Beat the egg as though you're going to scramble it. Just when you're really in the mood for breakfast, add the salt and bitters. It still looks good, right? Ruin that by adding the sugar. Keep whisking until you realize you're supposed to drink this. Add in the brandy and milk to try diluting the salty egg bitters. It won't work, but you'll feel better for trying. Drink the entire concoction as quickly as possible, then try to keep it all down with a brandy chaser. It may not cure your stomach ache, but it should make you sleepy enough to settle back into bed.

Roman Punch

12 Lemons
2 Oranges
8 cups Sugar
1 bottle Champagne
Whites of 8 Eggs

Zest the lemons and oranges. Mix the citrus zest with your 8 cups of sugar. Wait, that's not enough citrus! Go ahead and squeeze the lemons and oranges and mix their juice in with the sugar. Now wash your hands and go find something else to do for a day.

When you come back, strain the citrus sugar through cheesecloth. You'll end up with a dubious sugar citurs juice and a whole lot of discarded granules.

Feel free to combine the sugary remains with 1 cup of almond or coconut oil. You now have a citrussy sugar body scrub for your shower. The Victorians hadn't invented showers yet and were still only moderately comfortable with cleaning more than once a week, but you're welcome to pretend you're part of a well traveled, multicultural Steampunk airship with a Moorish captain who insists on positively decadent standards of personal hygiene.

Meanwhile, you still need a drink to help you recover from all that nearly pornographic talk of bathing. What is this world coming to?

Before you become faint from this lewd discussion, hurry to the kitchen for some wholesome work.

Beat the egg whites until they're frothy, but not yet fully stiff. Mix them with the strained citrus sugar juice. Once well blended, add the champagne and mix gently. Serve frothy result in a round champagne glass.

Coffee Cocktail

1 Egg
1 tsp Sugar
1 shot Port
2 shots Brandy

Oh, those Victorian jokesters! If you craved a cup of coffee but were trying to cut back on caffeine, they had a three shot cocktail to fool the eyes, if not the tongue. Allegedly, the mix of these ingredients looked like a cup of coffee on ice. After a couple glasses of the substitute, one would either pass out or start a bar fight. It was all worth it to avoid those pesky stimulants, right?

To mix this, fill a shaker half way with ice. Crack your egg into it, add everything else, and shake like you're trying to cold scramble your breakfast. Pour the result into a coffee mug full of ice and prepare for the look of un-caffeinated despair when you serve a depressant to someone craving their morning stimulant.

Brandy Egg Cloud

1 Egg
2 shots Heavy Cream
1 shot Brandy
2 tsp Sugar
Dash Vanilla Extract
Cinnamon

This is a lot like a single serving of egg nog. Fill a cocktail shaker half way with ice. Crack in your egg, add the brandy, sugar and vanilla, then hold the shaker near your belt and give it a good, enthusiastic shake.

When you remove the cap, the foamy white blend may enthusiastically spew forward. Assure people this is a sign of your bartending enthusiasm. Strain the remainder into a well iced lowball glass and sprinkle a dash of cinnamon on top. This is an excellent drink for a gentleman's club.

Whiskey Nog For Two

2 Eggs
2 shots Whiskey
2/3 cup Whole Milk
2 tsp Sugar
2 pinches Salt

Sometimes you don't want to make enough egg nog for a party. This is a great drink for curling up around a fire with that special someone, wishing electricity would be invented soon so you could see them better, and wondering when hemlines might rise above the ankle.

Whisk the egg until it looks ready to be scrambled. Add the sugar and beat it again. At this point, your arm is probably getting tired, so go ahead and dump everything else in your bowl and whisk away until it seems perfectly blended.

Alternately, you could just throw everything in a blender while watching a video of fire flicker across your television.

Some may find 2 shots of whiskey to be a little weak. Feel free to double both the whiskey and the sugar.

Empire in a Glass

1 Egg
1 shot Irish Whiskey
1 shot Rum
1/2 shot Gin
1/2 shot Vermouth
4 tsp Sugar
Juice of one Lemon

Think of this as the Long Island Iced Tea of its day. You put in a little bit of everything plus some cheap mixers and through the miracles of chemistry you ended up with a surprisingly palatable drink. In this case, modern drinkers may want to reduce the Vermouth down to a mere whisper while increasing the quantity of sugar.

Add all your ingredients to an icy cocktail shaker and beat it like you're oppressing ungrateful natives. Pour the result into a lightly iced lowball glass and pretend the middling amount of protein in the egg is enough to prevent you from getting drunk off three shots.

Rummy Egg

2 shots Rum
1 shot Brandy
1 tsp Sugar
1 Egg
Grated Nutmeg

Oh, those punsters! Make a Rummy Egg by dumping all your ingredients in a cocktail shaker and shaking it until you come up with a better pun or your arm gets tired. Strain it all into a well iced lowball glass, dust the top with some nutmeg, and write, "I'm already drunk" on your hand in sharpie. If you still remember writing on yourself in the morning, thank your bartender and your friends.

Claret Egg Cocktail

4 shots Claret
3 shots Whole Milk
2 tsp Sugar
1 Egg

The Victorians loved Claret. If you're not a fan, any medium bodied red wine will do. The end result looks bemusingly like a frothy cup of blood, making this an eye catching convention drink.

Crack your egg into a cocktail shaker half full of ice. Add your Claret, milk, and if you're feeling dangerous, double the amount of sugar listed above. Pound it like you're trying to force the last ounce of liquid from a desiccated corpse. Pour the mix into your choice of a clear glass or vampire themed coffee cup and go prowling for former Goths who graduated to Steampunk when they discovered the color brown

PUNCHES

You'll find most 19th century punch recipes began by having you boil some water, add some egg whites, then skim the resulting foam off the top. This is because the Victorians weren't suicidal. They may not have understood why, but experience taught them boiling their water had a direct impact on not dying the day after drinking it. Since rivers in every city of the era were scarily contaminated with the waste of shiny new industry (and humans, and everything else quietly dumped in the river by moonlight), those egg whites did a great job of binding to particulates and drawing them to the top of the pot where they could be easily skimmed off. Boiling killed anything else living in the water. It was a slow process, but it was effective.

If you trust your local drinking water, skip the punch recipe steps involving a minimum 20 minutes of boiling followed by skimming. Just make the simple syrup called for in most of these recipes and start dumping in your other ingredients. However, if you plan on bottling any of your concoctions or if you're just curious about what's really in your water, give the Victorian methods a try. You might be in for a scummy surprise.

You may also find the quantities of both Champagne and sugar in these recipes downright scandalous by modern standards. The Victorians had a sweet tooth rivaling our own. Once cheap sugar became widely available, people couldn't get enough of it. The quantities involved might have been a display of wealth a century earlier, but by the 19th century, they honestly just liked it that way. A southern style Arnold Palmer (1/3 black tea, 1/3 lemonade, 1/3 sugar) would've gone down a treat.

Champagne wasn't saved for special occasions and toasts. During much of the 19th century, you'll find it was used as cheap filler. When making these punches, don't spend more than $6 per bottle of Champagne. If anyone questions you, just tell them the excessive sweetness of cheap bubbly more closely mimics the flavor of period drinks. Sadly, you'll be right.

Orange Wine Punch

4 cups Spring Water
2 cups Sugar
6 Egg Whites
1/2 tsp Champagne Yeast (available at homebrew stores)
Juice of 3 Lemons
Juice of 12 Oranges
Zest of 6 Oranges
2 bottles White Wine, chilled

It's once more time to make some simple syrup. In a saucepan, dissolve 1 cup of sugar in the water and lemon juice. While you're waiting for that to come to a boil, whisk the egg whites and remaining cup of sugar until you achieve sweet white peaks. Once your lemon sugar comes to a boil, dump your egg sugar into it and continue whisking until it's nice and smooth.

I know what you're thinking. Don't just dump the egg whites into the boiling water. You'll end up with lemonade flavored egg drop soup.

Simmer your eggy, lemony sugary mix for another 20 minutes. Then turn off the heat and allow it to cool for 40 minutes. After that, skim off any scum that dares rise to the surface.

Once your water cools, add your Champagne yeast and orange juice. Put a clean piece of cheesecloth over the top of your pot and leave it to sit overnight at room temperature. Don't just put a lid on the pot. Your concoction needs to breathe.

Twenty four hours later, use the cheesecloth to carefully strain your mix. Add it to a punchbowl and spike it with two bottles of chilled white wine. If, for some reason, people don't finish it all off at the party, pour the remainder into a container with a tight lid. It should stay drinkable in the fridge for 2-3 days.

Fruited Punch

1 pint Strawberries, sliced
1 Pineapple, peeled, cored, and cut into chunks
2 Lemons, sliced into rounds
6 Oranges, sliced into rounds
1 bottle Brandy
1 bottle Sherry
1 bottle Madira wine
4 bottles Champagne
1/2 gallon tonic water

Two bottles of hard alcohol and five bottles of wine were expected to yield twenty servings of punch. If you've seen much Victorian cooking, you know that as often as not, they believed flavor could be damned in favor of displaying how many kinds of things you could mix together. Why serve a nice beefsteak when you can have a horrible pottage made from beef, pork, lamb, game hens, chicken, venison, and rabbit?

This punch follows that same logic. Why serve a nice Champagne spiked with brandy and a little fruit when you can throw in some Madira and sherry?

Making this is distressingly simple. Pour your brandy and sherry into a punchbowl. It's no loss. They're probably not your favorite liquors anyway.

Now sacrifice that bottle of Madira you'd been saving for a nice red sauce. Stare forlornly at your perfectly good Champagne (or at the $4 bottles you picked up because you knew their fate) then dump them in along with the tonic water. Give it all a good stir and float the fruit on top.

The best thing you can say about this punch is it will efficiently get a group of people drunk while also preventing scurvy.

Navy Punch

1 bottle White Rum
1 bottle Champagne
4 cups strong Black Tea
10 cups of Sugar
Juice and rind of 8 Lemons

Modern drinkers may think 1/2 cup of sugar per serving is a bit excessive. Pshaw! The Royal Navy at the height of the British Empire deserved nothing less than the most tooth rottingly delicious beverages.

Brew your hot, strong, black tea for a minimum of 10 minutes. Add the lemon juice, half of the lemon rind, and sugar. Mix them in until the sugar melts into a lovely molten candy, then keep stirring for half an hour.

In fact, if you're feeling extra spunky, after 30 minutes you can siphon off 1/4 cup for a little quick period candy. Carefully peel long strips of rind off your remaining 4 lemons, making sure you leave no white pulp. Soak the peels in the syrup overnight, then carefully leave them out on waxed paper to dry. Congratulations, you made simple candied lemon peels with a hint of tea.

Meanwhile, after half an hour of stirring your massive pot of black tea and lemon simple syrup, it's time to add the rum. Give that a good stir. Now pour everything into your punch bowl and top it off with a bottle of Champagne to give it a nice bit of effervescence.

If modern drinkers find this a bit overly sweet, feel free to either cut the sugar in half or, if you'd like a less aggressive drink (or you're an American), use eight cups of weaker tea brewed for only three minutes.

Hotpot

1/2 gallon old, stale Ale (not lager beer)
2 cups Gin
8 cups Sugar
5 Eggs
1 tbsp fresh Ginger
1/2 tsp fresh Nutmeg

Warm the ale in a saucepan, but don't bring it to a boil. Meanwhile, brutally beat the eggs until they cower into a soggy mass of protein. Sweeten them with the sugar, ginger and nutmeg, then remind them how bad they are by beating them again. Spare the rod, spoil the punch.

Pour your egg mix into your not-boiling ale. If the ale is too warm, you'll cook the eggs and end up with a horribly unpleasant texture as well as a crime against alcohol.

Aggressively whisk the egg mix until it's well integrated with the ale. Once the two of them are over their differences and appear to be getting along well, introduce the gin. Your aggressive whisking will make the ale, eggs and gin forget their differences as they vow to team up against you. In this way, you will create unity from diversity, much like the British Empire itself.

This is best served hot, in tumblers, while proudly gazing at a map of Britain's dominions.

Prince of Wales Punch

2 bottles Champagne
1 bottle Burgundy
1 bottle White Rum
10 Lemons
2 Oranges
12 cups Sugar

You could accurately follow the instructions to make this drink. Or you could save that bottle of Burgundy from a sugary demise. Only you can decide.

If you're feeling authentic, you'll begin with making citrus sugar. Squeeze the juice from your oranges and lemons, mix in the sugar, and allow it to sit under a veil of cheesecloth for 36 hours. Dump your citrus sugar in a punch bowl and add your alcohol. Mix well and let sit for the next 24 hours. Yes, of course your Champagne will go flat and your Burgundy will go stale. You'll probably also acquire some fascinated fruit flies who will dance happy drunken jigs on your cheesecloth.

Alternately, you could mix your citrus sugar in advance (it keeps for days). An hour or so before your party, dilute however much citrus sugar you deem appropriate (for example, four cups) in a punch bowl full of white rum. Then top it off with the two bottles of Champagne. Serve the Burgundy separately.

Half Dozen Punch

1 bottle Claret
1 wine glass Rum
1 wine glass Whiskey
1 wine glass Benedictine (or Cognac with 4 dashes bitters)
1 wine glass Peach Brandy
1 wine glass Gin
Juice of 3 Lemons
2 cups Tonic Water
1/2 cup Sugar
1 cup chopped Brandied Cherries or Brandied Peaches

Half Dozen Punch was intended to serve half a dozen alcohols to half a dozen people in one horrifying glass. This was the sort of light afternoon refreshment that went well with bread and butter or cucumber sandwiches. Any weak dandy who couldn't handle a wine glass full of hard alcohol didn't deserve the honor of an invitation to your afternoon get together.

In fitting with the light, casual refreshment, it was acceptable to simply dump all the ingredients into a punch bowl two hours before your party and stir. The flavors would have thoroughly mingled by the time guests arrived.

Real drinks would be served later, over dinner.

Victorian Wassail Punch

6 small Apples, washed and cored
1 gallon Hard Cider
1 Lemon
2 Cinnamon Sticks
6 Cloves
1/4 tsp Nutmeg

You need some real attention to detail to coax the flavor from this deceptively simple list of ingredients, but the result is worth it.

Preheat your oven to 375F. Wash and core your apples then cut a few vent slices into the middle. Bake them for 45-50 minutes, uncovered, until the apples have softened and the skins begin to split.

Meanwhile, heat your hard cider in a saucepan. Don't bring it to a boil. You want a nice warm cider. If you have a mortar and pestle, bruise your cinnamon sticks and cloves. Beating them with a heavy aluminum can will also work. Add in your spices and stir occasionally while you wait for your apples to bake.

Once the apples are cooked, go ahead and dump them into your spicy cider. Stir heartily until you have a nice apple mush with bits of skin floating in it. If any scum rises to the surface, carefully skim it off. Be careful not to remove your cinnamon sticks or cloves, though.

Serve hot, topped with a single slice of lemon.

This produces a hearty winter punch that warms your insides and delights your nose. For those of you who worry something so authentically tasty can't be Victorian, you're right. This is a much older recipe which they kept around out of holiday nostalgia, much like we do modern eggnog. I suggest we endeavor to bring it back into fashion.

Black and Tan Punch

2 bottles Champagne
An equal quantity of Guinness Stout
4 cups of Sugar
Juice of 6 Lemons
1 cup Brandied Cherries

This drink seems designed to equally insult lovers of beer, Champagne, and lemonade. Simply mix all five ingredients in a large punch bowl and serve over ice.

If you're in the mood to start a bare knuckles boxing match between two fine mustachioed gentlemen, this drink seems like a good start.

Victoria Punch

1 bottle Rum
1 empty rum bottle filled with Water
Juice of 8 Limes
6 dashes Bitters
1 cup Sugar
1 tsp Nutmeg

When in doubt, name your drink after the queen - even if your drink includes an ingredient as petty and dangerous as actual water. Considering how long she survived, it's doubtful Victoria actually drank water more than a few times in her life, but it's nice for the common people to think they have at least one thing in common with their queen. They're entirely wrong, but it's still a nice thought.

Empty the bottle of rum into a saucepan. Refill your bottle with water and empty that into the same saucepan. Bring it to a boil and add the sugar and lime juice. Boil for at least five minutes, stirring until the sugar completely dissolves. Add the nutmeg and bitters.

Stir well, cover with cheesecloth, and allow to sit for 48 hours before serving.

Majestic Victoria Punch

8 cups Water
4 cups Sugar
Juice of 8 Lemons
Juice of 4 Oranges
Rind of 2 Oranges
1 bottle Riesling
Hard English Cider equal to the quantity of wine
1/2 cup Gin

Much like Victoria herself, the full majesty of the empire was represented in this drink then sweetened by some blonde German loving.

Boil the water, add the sugar, and keep stirring until the sugar fully melts. Add the lemon juice, orange juice, and orange rind to the sugar mix, give it one more good stir, then take the pot off the heat and go find something else to do while it cools to room temperature.

When you come back, pour your room temperature citrus water into a punchbowl and mix in the Riesling, hard cider, and gin.

This makes a sweet, surprisingly refreshing drink with a crisp citrus flavor destined to confuse anyone who thinks 7-Up is made from actual lemons and limes.

Regent's Punch

8 cups Water
2 heaping tablespoons of loose Green Tea leaves
4 large Lemons
2 cups Sugar
1 bottle Champagne

Once up on a time green tea was a ridiculously expensive indulgence. Throwing in into a big pot of booze was a delightful extravagance. Today, you can get a drinkable green tea at a dollar store. Don't let that stop you from making this cocktail. It's actually one of the tastiest punches.

Throw the tea leaves into the water and bring them to a boil. While you're waiting, zest the outer portion of the lemons then carefully peel the fruit so it separates from the bitter white interior. Throw the white away then add the peeled fruit segments and exterior zest to your boiling pot of water. Let everything boil merrily for about ten minutes.

While the mix is still hot, strain out all the solids. Add the sugar and stir until it's pretty much melted. Pour that mix into a punchbowl then go about your business for the rest of the day. Just before your guests arrive, uncork the Champagne and pour it into the tea.

Think of this as the early British rendition of a Mimosa. It makes an equally light, refreshing morning cocktail for those people who can't wait until after 5 to start their drinking.

Loyal Legion Punch

4 gallons Whiskey
1 gallon Rum
1/2 gallon Cherry Cordial
100 Limes
12 Lemons
6 Oranges
3 Pineapples
10 pounds Sugar
4 bottles Champagne
1 new, large, clean plastic trashcan

Nothing keeps a legion more loyal than getting them so drunk they forget what country they're fighting in. It's not clear whether this punch was meant to be served to bolster courage before the men went into battle or as a reward to the survivors. Either way, it's a potent forgetting potion.

You won't find a better period drink for a convention or party. This can be made in a (fresh, clean, new) trashcan on Friday, allowed to steep until Saturday, and serve up to impressed masses. Best yet, you can also easily make it do double duty steeping alcoholic fruit to be served separately, you clever thing.

Find some minions willing to peel and juice your 100 limes. Don't buy a bunch of squeezy plastic limes full of horrifying concentrate from the grocery store. They really will ruin the all natural flavor of this drink. Put on a DVD, get a cutting board, and peel until you never want to see another citrus again. You'll want the peels of 20 limes and the juice of them all. These go into your fresh trashcan. Next, peel and juice your lemons and oranges. Everything but the nasty white interior goes into the bucket.

I know what you're thinking. The white citrus interior can't be that bad. It would be so much easier to just chop the fruit into quarters, throw it in the bucket, and mash it with a shovel. Resist the temptation. However bad you think it might be, that nasty bitter interior is infinitely worse. You don't want to ruin five gallons of booze the night before a party. Be patient.

Once you're done zesting and juicing, add your whiskey, rum and cherry cordial to the bucket and give it a good stir. Go ahead and use mid to low grade booze here. You're about to add in ten pounds of sugar. That'll cover up anything.

You can be forgiven if you decide to cut the sugar back to, say, a mere five pounds. It's still enough. However much you add, dump it in and give it a good stir. A broom handle works well at this point.

Core and skin your pineapples. You want to cut the result into nice, edible sized chunks. If you want to serve a mildly alcoholic fruit platter, go pick up some nice porous fruits like honeydew, cantaloupe, watermelon, or strawberries. Peel all your fruit into nice bite sized pieces and dump it into a thin cheesecloth bag. You can skip this step if you want to spend an hour carefully fishing fruit out of your punch. It's up to you. Throw the bag (or just the fruit) into your trash can, close the lid, and forget about it. If you're curious how it's doing, you can always give it another stir once or twice. This punch is best left soaking for a minimum of 24 hours, though you can leave it for up to 3 days with no problem.

The day you're going to serve it, first fish out the floating fruit. Don't worry about the citrus peel. That will add a jaunty color, plus icebreaker evidence of all your hard work. Arrange the fruit neatly on serving platters. You now look like you went to tremendous trouble to make a barrel of punch and some infused fruit. Bask in the admiration.

Ten minutes before the party starts, give the punch one last hearty stir then add the Champagne. Anything more than $6 a bottle is a waste. You should be adding sweet, alcoholic fizz to your still punch. Give it one more gentle stir. You can offer your guests ice or serve it at room temperature. Either way, you should now have enough authentic 19th century booze to inebriate an entire legion and perhaps inspire some bold romantic conquests.

State of Schuyhill Punch

1 gallon Rum
1/2 gallon Peach Brandy
4 gallons Water
3 pounds Sugar
20 Lemons or Limes

This is another fairly straightforward punch intended to serve large quantities of booze to undiscriminating audiences who like their sugar. Start by doing your best to dissolve the sugar into the water. Once you've lost your patience, go ahead and add the rum and peach brandy.

Stare at your lemons or limes in frustration, then resign yourself to the fact that you have a lot of peeling and juicing ahead of you. Zest or peel your citrus so only the colored potion falls into your precious pot of sugary booze. When you're left with nothing but a bald white pile of fruit, cut the pieces in half and juice them into the pot. Give it another good stir, put a lid on it, and leave it overnight.

Meanwhile, roughly chop up a few of your reaming citrus halves. Mix them with two cups of ice and slowly force them into your garbage disposal. This will clean out some of the congealed grease and leave it smelling fresh and clean. You're welcome.

Celebrate your Martha Stewart-like skills the next day by indulging in a big glass of Schuyhill Punch poured over ice. If you're feeling extra fancy, garnish the bowl with cherries right before serving.

Hot Cranberry Tea Punch

1 gallon Brandy
8 tbsp Black Tea leaves
4 cups boiling Water
2 cups unsweetened Cranberry Juice
2 bottles Hard Apple Cider
1/2 cup Sugar
2 Cinnamon Sticks
4 Cloves
1 inch fresh Ginger, peeled and diced

Put your water in a good sized pot. While it's heating up, dice your fresh peeled ginger and throw it in the water. Smash the cinnamon sticks using the canned goods of your choice in order to bruise the spices and release the flavors. Before they can recover from their injuries, throw them in the water.

Once the water comes to a boil, throw in your tea leaves. If you don't have loose tea, you can always throw in 8 teabags. No one is watching. Turn off the heat, put a lid on the pot, and let it sit on your cooling burner for the next ten minutes.

Strain the solids from your strong spicy tea. To keep the liquid from getting too lonely, introduce it to it's new sugary friend. Once the sugar has happily melted into the tea, introduce the cranberry juice, hard cider, and brandy. Give them a gentle stir so the flavors will play nicely together.

Leave the mix over a very low heat or pour the punch into a crockpot to keep it warm. Serve with a dusting of nutmeg or cinnamon.

Pine-Apple Punch

1 gallon yesterday's leftover Black Tea
1 gallon Apple Juice
1/2 gallon Pineapple Juice
1/2 gallon Rum
1/2 gallon Whiskey

Feel free to stare in awe. This is one of the few, rare recipes that doesn't include any sugar. Sure, it has two kinds of juice, but that wouldn't normally stop the Victorians from adding some of their precious white grains of goodness to anything they put in their mouths.

This punch is simplicity itself. Put everything in a bowl. Stir it up then serve it up. If you're either feeling fancy or don't happen to have leftover tea sitting around from last night, you can always brew a fresh gallon.

If you can find fresh squeezed apple juice - the kind that looks like deliciously chunky brown apple cider - you'll enjoy a wonderfully different flavor from the urine colored transparent sugar water sold as "juice" in most grocery stores. In fact, it's better to replace the apple juice with fresh apple cider than use any apple juice you can see through.

This is equally good as a warm winter drink or poured over ice during the last days of summer.

Lime Rum Punch

4 cups Water
3 cups Rum
2 cups Sugar
20 Limes
4 dashes Bitters
Nutmeg for dusting

For once you're spared the misery of zesting twenty limes. Instead, you merely need to juice them. Huzzah!

Squeeze the essence of your limes into a large pitcher. Add the water and sugar, then stir until the sugar dissolves. Add in your rum and bitters and give it another stir. If there's any room left in the pitcher, fill it to the top with ice. If not, settle for serving it over ice. Dust the top with some aromatic nutmeg and enjoy what amounts to a mintless Victorian mojito.

Plain Punch

1/2 gallon Rum
1/2 gallon Brandy
1/2 gallon Water
6 cups Sugar
4 Lemons
1/2 tsp Nutmeg

Wait, only six cups of sugar? Only two kinds of alcohol? Only one spice? This was poverty punch indeed.

Zest your lemons. After all, if you're drinking this, you can't afford to waste anything.

While you're busy zesting, bring the water to a boil. Add your sugar, the juice of your four lemons, and your precious lemon zest. All you're left with now are bitter white cores and a burning sensation in your fingertips, which you no doubt deserve for the crime of being poor.

Once the sugar melts, take the pot off the stove and wait for the contents to cool. This is a good time to watch paint dry while contemplating the misery of your life. You could just drink the rum or brandy straight, but you already went to all this effort. Be patient. Soon you'll have enough plain punch to make all the bad thoughts go away for one more night.

Whenever you believe it has reached a drinkable temperature, add your alcohols and give the punch a good stir. Toast the fact that you and your family probably won't die of river poisoning tonight, then drink up until you pass out.

Lavender Victorian Lemonade

6 cups Water
3 cups Gin
2 cups fresh Lemon Juice
1 cup Sugar
12 stems of fresh Lavender

Victorian ladies are often given an entirely undeserved reputation for sternness and sobriety. Elite cultural ideals written by a small minority paint one picture. Recipes paint another.

A respectable punch to be served at a light luncheon for ladies included half a cup of gin per person. Keep that in perspective the next time someone complains one bottle of champagne is too much alcohol for half a dozen mimosas.

To make this aggressively floral punch, start by boiling the water. Add the sugar and stir until it completely dissolves. Now add your lavender, give it a good stir, then put a lid on the pot and take it off the heat. Let this steep for about an hour. You now have lavender simple syrup.

If you think you'll want to use lavender simple syrup in other drinks, feel free to double or triple the recipe. Keep the syrup in an airtight container in a cool, dark place. It'll stay good until it starts to crystallize, which could take months depending on your climate.

If you're a green tea drinker, this is a nice substitute for honey.

Once your lavender simple syrup has steeped for an hour, carefully strain away all the solids. Add your lemon juice and gin, give it a good stir, and set it out for the ladies. This can be served on ice or at room temperature. If you have spare lavender, use it as a garnish.

Charles Dickens Very Own Christmas Punch

1/2 gallon bottled Mineral Water
1 large (750 ml) bottle Dark Rum
1 small (350 ml) bottle Brandy
2 cups Brown Sugar
3 large Lemons
Cinnamon Sticks
Grated Nutmeg

Gently warm your rum and brandy in a saucepan. The goal is to warm it up, not boil off the alcohol. When it's unpleasantly warm to the touch, add in the sugar and stir until it dissolves. Once the sugar granules are nothing but a ghost of sweetness past, add in the zest and juice of your lemons. Let this simmer gently on the stove for ten minutes. Just before serving, remove it from the heat and add the bottled mineral water.

If you're feeling fancy, you can cut out a wheel of lemon to put at the bottom of each glass. Fill the glass with punch, spike the lemon with a cinnamon stick, and top it with a sprinkle of nutmeg.

Dickens described the cinnamon, nutmeg, and lemon wheels as optional, so feel free to experiment to find a flavor you like.

Since Dickens did have a flare for the dramatic, he also offered an alternate serving method.

Instead of pouring his punch into individual glasses, bring it to the table and pour it into a large, fire-proof bowl. The last part is important if you don't want to be drinking liquid plastic.

Float a ladle full of brandy on top of the punch. Refill the ladle with Brandy and carefully ignite the surface. Ever so slowly, pour the flaming brandy into the punchbowl. If all goes well, your waterfall of flame will set the punch in the bowl on fire. If not, you'll look a bit pretentious, but under the circumstances, no one will be terribly surprised.

Extinguish the flames by giving the bowl a good, hearty stir, then ladle your warm, no longer flaming drink into glasses prepared with your choice of lemon wheels or cinnamon sticks. Once everyone has a glass in hand, it's time for some ghost stories.

TEA COCKTAILS

When reading through older English recipes, you'll find "Tea" didn't always mean the black or green leaves we enjoy today. Basically, it's an old word for "anything we can boil in water long enough to leech out some flavor." Yes, anything. There are late night tummy soother recipes for Beef Tea made from squeezing the blood out of a room temperature steak.

These drinks are tastier.

For one thing, most of them actually involve caffeine bearing leaves instead of cow blood. For another, they're all fortified with enough sugar to put a soft drink to shame. If you ignore the actual quantity of alcohol you could almost pretend these are stimulating, sugary Victorian Energy Drinks meant to keep you awake through a scintillating lecture on new uses for electricity. Really, though, they were the Red Bull and Vodka cocktails of their day.

When brewing your base tea, feel free to liberally adjust how long the leaves spend in the water. Modern Americans typically prefer tea brewed for one to three minutes. At five, they find it undrinkably bitter. The Victorians, on the other hand, preferred a strong ten minute brew.

Tea cocktails make a fine addition to any Steampunk gathering. If you're feeling civilized, serve them with ginger biscuits and cucumber sandwiches. If you're fresh from repairing the engines of your airship, enjoy these fine drinks with cold meats, a thick wedge of cheese, and a hunk of dark bread.

Blueberry Tea

6 shots cold, pre-made Blueberry Tea
1 shot Amaretto
1/2 shot Grand Marnier (or other orange liqueur)

Brew whatever blueberry tea catches your eye. I prefer Celestial Seasonings. It's not authentically Victorian, but neither is good hygiene.

If you're in the mood for a sipping drink, fill a highball glass half way with ice, add the Amaretto and Grand Marnier, then top it off with the blueberry tea. If you're in the mood for something stronger, add the alcohol and ice to a lowball glass and top off with notably less tea. If you need to sweeten it up, add a dash of honey.

Bourbon Slush

7 cups Water
3 cups Bourbon Whiskey
2 cups strong Black Tea
1 1/2 cups Sugar
Juice of 6 large Lemons
Juice of 6 small Oranges (Clementine's preferred)

The Victorians absolutely loved shaved ice. If you're feeling mildly authentic, get a cheap Hawaiian Shaved Ice machine and substitute that for the water. If your passion for authenticity borders on OCD, get a ten pound block of ice and a chisel.

For those of you using the ice shaver, mix your bourbon, brewed tea, sugar, lemon juice and orange juice until the sugar has been tamed from angry crystals to meek citizens of your alcoholic realm. Whenever you serve a cocktail, add a generous scoop of ice to a lowball glass and douse it with about 1/3 cup of the bourbon mix. Remember that while the Victorians would've considered this a perfectly good treat for children, the current constabulary heartily disagree.

For those of you who aren't ashamed to abuse modern contrivances for the sake of convenience, mix everything in a bucket and put it in the freezer. Don't skimp on the water. Your alcohol won't freeze, so you need the liquid in order to get a good slush texture. Remove it from the freezer no more than half an hour before serving. If it froze too much, go ahead and blend some to make it slushier. Transfer the contents of your bucket to a punch bowl to add a little class.

If you're an entirely lazy bastard, buy a bag of crushed ice from the grocery store and substitute 12 well packed cups for the 7 cups of water. At this point, you might as well be honest with yourself and your guests by serving it in plastic Solo Cups.

Believer's Rum Tea

4 shots cold, Black Tea
1 1/2 shots Dark Rum
1/2 shot Dark Creme de Cacao
2 tsp Sugar
Juice of 1/2 Lemon

Sugar is not a friend to cold drinks. Classy people with a bit of free time resort to simple syrups. Lazy people with a bit of muscle just put everything in a cocktail shaker and attempt to beat an invisible leviathan to death.

If you want to take the simple syrup route, mix the tea, lemon juice, and sugar in a small saucepan and bring it to a boil. Stir well. Continue stirring until the sugar has entirely melted and the mix has lost all graininess. Now let it cool, add your rum and Creme de Cacao, and serve in a highball glass full of ice.

For the faster muscle bound route, add all your ingredients to a cocktail shaker full of ice. Shake with a worrisome power and vigor, then strain into a highball glass full of ice. Your drink will be grainier than the simple syrup version, so you might as well drink two to make up for it. You won't notice as much difference when quaffing the second drink.

Colonial Boy

5 shots hot Black Tea
1 shot Irish Whiskey
1 tsp Sugar
1 dash Bitters

Boys must've been bitter about spending time in the colonies. This simple hot drink is basically nothing more than a good cup of tea ruined with a dash of bitters and enlivened by a shot of whiskey. Try doubling the sugar. Or, better yet, simply sniff the bitters bottle, put the cap back on, and drink your whiskey spiked tea in peace.

Fireside Tea

5 shots hot Black Tea
1 shot Dark Rum
1 Lemon Wedge
1 Cinnamon Stick
1 tsp Sugar

This is suspiciously similar to a hot toddy made with rum instead of bourbon.

Make a mug of hot black tea. Add your sugar, rum, and a well squeezed lemon wedge, then stir heartily with the cinnamon stick. In 2 minutes, remove the lemon wedge (otherwise it will start to turn the drink unnecessarily bitter.) Leave the cinnamon stick in place and relax with your drink.

If you decide you need a few more warm beverages to get you through the night, you can reuse the same cinnamon stick at least a dozen times. If it starts to lose flavor, ask someone sober to gently grate the exterior in order to remove the tea saturated part and give you access to fresher bits of bark.

Gunfire Tea

5 shots strong Black Tea
1 shot Dark Rum
1/2 shot Molasses
Dash Bitters
Dash Fine Fireplace Ash

Look, we all know fire cleanses things. You boil water to make it safe to drink. You cook meat to make it safe to eat. It only makes sense that if you burn wood the resulting ash would be edible, right?

My theory is once upon a time, a clumsy soldier mucked up the tea, tried to hide the flavor, and then bluffed so convincingly his creation became a requested drink.

To mix this distinctive cocktail, first grind any lumps out of your ash. It should be grey and silky. Add it to the hot tea and stir until the ash nearly disappears. You want to get it into a suspension before adding the molasses. Otherwise, you're going to have a disgusting coal flavored candy lump at the bottom of your otherwise mediocre tea. Once it's all smooth, enjoy this 19th century soldier's beverage while pretending to be an armchair general from the future.

Hot Tea Toddy

5 shots hot Black Tea
2 shots Bourbon
1 tbsp Honey
1 thick slice of Lemon
1 Cinnamon Stick

A real hot toddy doesn't need tea to water it down. However, the British never met a beverage they thought couldn't be improved with a few leaves.

Brew your tea. Add the bourbon, squeeze in the lemon juice, and top it off with the honey. Use the cinnamon stick to mix it until the honey melts. Leave the cinnamon stick steeping while the tea cools. There's no point leaving in the lemon wedge. It'll only add bitterness to the tea while sucking up the sticky honey.

As with the Fireside Tea, you can easily dry and reuse your cinnamon stick swizzler.

Iced Lemonade Tea

10 cups Tea
10 large Lemons
2 cups Clear Rum
1 cup Sugar
Ice

Brew your tea in a small soup pot.

While the Tea is brewing, attempt to peel the rind off your lemons. You don't actually need this. It just makes a nice garnish. Plus, it gives you the illusion of doing something productive while you're literally waiting for water to boil.

Once the tea is ready, strain the leaves, return the tea to the pot, and bring it back to a boil. Add the sugar. Stir frantically, as though you've made some terrible mistake that you can magically clear away so no one will notice. If you keep this up for awhile, the sugar will miraculously dissolve and all evidence of offending grains will disappear. Congratulations!

Now add the rum and the juice of the 10 lemons. Stir a bit more, just for good measure.

Depending on your patience, you can either put the pot of tea in the fridge and wait for it to cool down or you can pack highball glasses with ice and carefully pour in your mix. Either way, garnish the glass with some of your lemon peelings and enjoy some heartily alcoholic lemonade.

Orange Tea

5 shots hot Black Tea
1 shot White Rum
1 shot Cointreau or other orange liqueur
1 tsp Sugar

You could do something completely novel with this - say, garnish it with a slice of orange to add some natural flavor. But no, in a world of citrus spiked alcoholic tea beverages, that would make too much sense. Instead, this is a great excuse to add an expensive ingredient you'll barely be able to taste. Take that, lower classes!

Have your servants make a nice mug of tea. Once the tea is ready, they should dissolve a teaspoon of sugar in it, add a shot each of rum and Cointreau, and pause briefly to wonder why you have scurvy when you drink all these lovely citrus flavored beverages. Don't worry. A couple mugs of Orange Tea will make you forget about all the pain from your bleeding gums and fingernails.

Indian Tea

5 shots hot Black Tea
1 shot Gold Rum
1/2 shot Amaretto
1 tsp Orange Zest
1 tsp Sugar

Neither Indians nor Native Americans had a penchant for drinks made with rum and amaretto, but that never stopped the British from assigning a liberal hand in naming. This could just as easily be China Tea or Siam Tea (although in those cases I'd recommend adding star anise and a cinnamon stick.)

This is yet another drink where one simply makes a nice hot mug of tea then dumps in some alcohol, sugar and a random flavoring agent. Let your finished boozy tea steep for at least five minutes in order to leach a nice aroma from the orange zest.

That also gives it enough time to cool so you won't burn the top of your mouth, leading to a horrifying cycle of drinking more cups of Indian Tea, faster each time, in order to numb the pain by killing more nerve endings and dousing your brain in alcohol. After nineteen cups you'll wake up belowdecks on a ship you've never seen before, smelling of fish, with a full bladder, an empty wallet, and no idea whether you're on a friendly river cruise, a reality show, or a deep sea arctic fishing vessel. The moral of the story is you really need to let the orange peels steep.

Masala Chai Toddy

3 tsp Black Tea Leaves
3 cups Water
1/2 inch piece fresh Ginger
3 - 4 crushed Cardamom Pods
3 whole Cloves
1 Cinnamon Stick
1 - 2 whole Black Peppercorns
4 tsp Sugar
1 cup Brandy
1 cup Milk

Bring the water to a boil. Add the tea, ginger, cardamom, cloves, cinnamon, and peppercorns to the pot and stir well. Put a lid on the pot, remove it from the heat, and let it sit for 15 minutes.

That's right, Americans. Fifteen minutes. If you don't like the flavor, you can always use this strong, dark tea to stain wood.

Assuming your only ambition is staining your teeth, strain all the solids out of your frightfully strong tea. Weaken it up a bit by dousing it in milk and sugar, then put a little hair on its chest with the brandy. Stir well, pour into a respectable teapot, and serve in small, delicate teacups with a side of digestive biscuits.

Indian Masala Chai

4 cups Water
4 tsp Black Tea Leaves
1 Cinnamon Stick
8 Cardamom Pods
8 Whole Cloves
1 cup Rum
1 cup Whole Milk
4 tbsp Sugar

This is rather obviously similar to the last recipe except they've substituted peppercorns for proportionately more sugar. This is a good deal for everyone.

Bring the water to a boil. Add the tea leaves, cinnamon, cardamom and cloves. Cover, turn the heat to low, and simmer for 10 minutes. Yes, this is a weaker tea made with more water and less booze. You can smell the first stirrings of the temperance movement in this spicy brew.

Remove the tea from the heat and strain it into a teapot. Add the milk, sugar and demon rum, then stir well. The original recipe said one couldn't imbibe enough of this concoction to actually get drunk. Steampunks, you have a challenge.

Russian Tea

8 tsp Black Tea Leaves
8 cups Water
Juice of 8 large Oranges
Juice of 1 large Lemon
2 cups Pineapple Juice
2 cups Brandy
1 cup sugar
8 Whole Cloves

We continue our Tea World Tour with a stop in a northern nation where it is impossible to grow citrus fruit. This recipe summarizes everything you need to know about the average 19th century tea drinker's knowledge of geography.

Fill a good sized pot with everything but the Brandy and bring it to a boil. Turn down the heat and let it simmer for at least half an hour, stirring occasionally. When you're ready to serve, add the two cups of Brandy and an apology to your dentist.

Lime Tea

1 gallon strong Black Tea
4 cups Arrack (substitute spiced rum if you can't find
Arrack)
3 cups Sugar
20 Limes
Freshly Ground Nutmeg

Prepare your tea however you like, as long as you end up with a gallon of it. Bring that gallon of tea to a boil and add the three cups of sugar. Boil, stirring frequently, until the sugar melts into the tea. Yes, you're making something suspiciously close to a black tea simple syrup. This is normally the part where I'd tell you to save some in order to use it in a dessert or furniture stain, but honestly, unless you're making tea concentrate to last you through some post apocalyptic nightmare, there's not much you can do with black tea simple syrup other than booze it up.

Therefore, while the sugar is melting into your tea, juice all 20 of those limes and squeeze them right into the tea mix. Don't even think of doing something foolish like buying a plastic squeezy lime from the grocery store and emptying it into the mix instead. If you're contemplating that path, you might as well just add a few dashes of bitters to some Mountain Dew.

Once your sugar is melted and your lime juice is integrated, add your Arrack. If you can't get a hold of Arrack, go ahead and substitute golden spiced rum. It's not the same, but since you don't know what Arrack tastes like, you won't know any better. It'll still end up tasty.

Somehow, this drink ended up one of the rare tea beverages best served cold. Relish the novelty. Refrigerate it until you're ready to serve then pour it into lowball glasses full of ice. If you're feeling fancy, garnish with half of a juiced lime.

Artillery Punch

1 gallon strong Black Tea
4 cups Orange Juice
4 cups Rye Whiskey
4 cups Dark rum
2 cups Brandy
Juice of 6 Lemons
1 750 ml bottle Red Wine
1 shot Bitter Herbal Liqueur or 10 dashes Bitters

Caffeine, Vitamin C and enough alcohol to pickle your eyeballs would've made any artilleryman happy to see this punch. The instructions are quite simple. Put everything into a giant bowl and stir it up. If it's not sweet enough, add more orange juice.

It's rare these days to find a recipe where whiskey and rum are the fillers and fruit juices are merely present to add a splash of color. If your liver can't stand the authentic 19th century assault, try doubling the quantity of tea (and perhaps halving the quantity of alcohol.) You can also considerably modify the flavor by saving the bottle of red wine for its own occasion instead of leaving it to viciously fight against the assault of citrus and hard alcohol.

RUM COCKTAILS

Rum is the saucy drink of choice for your Steampunk sky pirate. Those of you seeking an authentic Victorian flavor need to search the cheapest, bottom rotgut shelves of your local liquor store. The $6 gallon bottle will still be too refined and palatable, so try adding a nice mix of rat droppings, sweat scraped from a homeless man's armpit, and the bitter white citrus interior you've thrown away from all the other recipes in this book. It'll still be too pure for the sake of authenticity, but you'll start to get a feeling for why every rum cocktail of the 19th century was blended with citrus, sugar, and crushing regret.

The classic rum drink was a Shrub. This was essentially equal parts sugar, citrus, dear-god-please-cut-the-flavor, and sadly, rum. The point was to get a large group of people drunk as efficiently as possible with a minimum of expense. In other words, these are great party drinks.

Ship's Rum Shrub

120 gallons Rain Water
60 gallons Rum
8 gallons Lemon Juice
6 gallons Orange Juice
2 pounds Lemon Rind
1 pound Orange Rind
100 pounds White Sugar
40 Cinnamon Sticks
10 Nutmegs

Fill a wooden barrel with the rum, lemon rind, and orange rind. Cover it to keep the bugs out and come back in a couple days. Add the lemon juice, orange juice, sugar and bruised spices. Set a boy to mixing well. Gather the men and divide the mix between six barrels. Add ten gallons of rum to each barrel then top it off with good, clean rain water. Bung the barrels and roll them around in order to mix everything well. Let the barrels sit for another day then drink. Add more sugar if it's not sweet enough or more lemon juice if you can still taste the rum.

Steampunk sky pirates wanting to serve an authentic beverage to their crew could easily cut the quantities down to 10%. Since even the harshest rum available today is smoother than anything the Victorians produced, perhaps spare your crew's teeth by cutting the sugar down to 5%.

For those of you seeking an incredibly cheap version to make at a Steampunk convention, you can find the following at your corner Walgreens.

2 gallons of the cheapest Dark Rum you can find
4 gallons of Tap Water
2 gallons of store bought Lemonade
1 gallon store bought Orange Juice
4 tbsp ground Nutmeg
10 Cinnamon Sticks
1 ten gallon trash can

If you buy the cheapest store brand juices you shouldn't need all the extra sugar. Beat the cinnamon sticks with the back of an aluminum can (save time by doing this while you're still in the store). If they don't have cinnamon sticks, add 4 tbsp ground cinnamon to the mix. If they don't have nutmeg, learn to live without it. Throw everything into your trash can, stir mightily, and serve in classy red Solo cups. It'll still taste better than any shrub made in the 19th century.

Raisin Rum Shrub

5 gallons Rum
2 gallons Raisin Wine
4 cups Orange Flower Water
Juice of 10 Lemons
6 cups Sugar

Both raisin wine and orange flower water were once cheap filler ingredients which are now prohibitively expensive. If you're looking for a strong, unusual flavor of the period, though, it might be worth poking around your local brand of Booze Warehouse.

The instructions are quite simple - mix everything in a wooden barrel, bung it closed, roll it about, and let it sit for the next 10 days. If you're easily bored, roll the barrel once or twice a day while you're waiting.

People making this in a freshly purchased disposable plastic trash can will discover a faint plastic flavor after 10 days. You can mask it lightly and add a bit more authentic flavor by adding two cups of wood chips to the mix. Yes, really. You can find these in the BBQ section of your local superstore or Home Depot. Avoid hickory.

Liquodilla

1 gallon of the cheapest Rum
8 Lemons
6 Oranges
3 pounds Sugar
3 gallons Water

Zest the oranges and lemons. Add the peel to a gallon of rum and let it steep for 3 days.

Once your rum has had time to get extra friendly with the citrus peels, boil the 3 gallons of water and add the 3 pounds of sugar. Let it boil for at least half an hour, stirring frequently to dissolve the sugar. Skim off any scum that floats to the top.

Let the water cool to room temperature. Now add the juice from five oranges and seven lemons. You can use the remaining lemons for garnish. Eat the leftover orange. Next, add in the rum. If you're feeling authentic, you'll let this sit for six weeks before drinking it. Honestly, though, do you think anyone desperate enough to drink a cup of dissolved sugar in every glass of Liquodilla was going to wait a month and a half? Heck no. You can keep it that long if you're not serving it at a party, but honestly, once you mix in the rum the flavor doesn't change significantly. You've waited three days. Go get drunk.

Lingonberry Shrub

1/2 gallon Lingonberry Juice
2 gallons mid-grade White Rum
1/2 pound Brown Sugar
12 oz bottle Hard Apple Cider
4 bruised Cinnamon Sticks

The Norse brought many things in their conquest of the new world. Their most recent innovation was the mighty pine palace of Ikea. Anyone ready to set sail from that temple of pre-fabricated delight into a mysterious new world of deciphering cryptograms is best fortified by a drink inspired by those mighty blonde warriors.

Mix the brown sugar into your mid grade white rum until you run out of patience or it seems mostly dissolved, whichever comes first. Take out some of your Ikea furniture building resentment on the cinnamon sticks, then callously throw them into whatever unholy vat you're using to mix this concoction. Stir in everything else and blend while you glare at your prefab furniture instructions.

Store the mix at room temperature for at least one day. That should give you enough time to finish constructing your furniture. Invite people over to celebrate your Norse pine conquest with a hearty iced adult beverage.

Currant Shrub

6 cups Currant Juice
1 gallon Dark Rum
1 pound White Sugar
2 tbsp Nutmeg

Currant juice is another one of those oddball ingredients you may have difficulty finding. If you do stumble across some and wonder what to do with it, mixed drinks are always the answer.

Once more, simply mix everything until well blended. Walk away. You have better things to do with your life. If you're feeling curious, come back once a day to give it a stir. After 2-3 days the flavors should be well mingled. If you have a strong sweet tooth, keep the original quantity of sugar. Since both the rum and juice will be of a higher quality than anything available in the 19th century, feel free to cut the sugar in half.

Raspberry Shrub

2 gallons Dark Rum
1 gallon Brandy
1/2 gallon Raspberry Juice (alternately 4 pounds
frozen raspberries)
2 Oranges
1 pound Sugar

Raspberry juice is hard to find, so if it's unavailable pick up 4 pounds of frozen raspberries and throw them in a food processor or blender until they're nothing more than the blood red, pulpy memory of fruit. You could hydrate and strain the result to get half a gallon of juice. Alternately, if you enjoy a few pips in your teeth to give a drink both some substance and a fleeting hint of healthiness, just dump your gory mess into your rum.

Mix in the brandy, the sugar, and the zest and juice of your oranges. Let it sit in the refrigerator for a couple of days before serving over ice.

Nelson's Blood Cocktail

3 shots Champagne
1 shot Dark Rum
1 shot Port
1 shot Brandy
1 shot Blood Orange Juice
Blood Orange Slice

After all these shrubs, punches, and nogs, it's finally time for an actual cocktail! Like today, most people went to bars with friends. They'd all have a few ladles full of whatever punch the bar was serving that night. Cocktails were for pretentious loners too good to drink from the communal bowl and too anti-social to care.

Add your rum, port, brandy, and blood orange juice to a cocktail shaker and beat it like you're pulping Nelson's brains. Pour the result into a tall glass. Carefully float some chilled Champagne on top and garnish it with a slice of blood orange.

This is a strong, bitter, unsatisfying drink which will leave you angry in the morning, much like Nelson's campaigns.

Rum Sour

2 shots White Rum
Juice of 1 Lemon
1/2 shot Simple Syrup
Orange Slice

This is a simple, unpretentious, one dimensional drink. If you're in the mood for something boring, fill a lowball glass with ice. Add your rum, lemon juice and simple syrup to a cocktail shaker and shake like the sheer power of your muscles can magically transform the contents into a better drink. Pour the result over your ice and glare sadly before drinking.

Hot Buttered Rum

1 gallon Rum
1 pound Light Brown Sugar
1/2 pound Unsalted Butter (two sticks)
3 tsp Vanilla
2 tsp Ground Cinnamon
2 tsp Ground Nutmeg
1/2 tsp Ground Allspice

If you're honest with yourself you'll start making a batch of cookies while you're preparing your hot buttered rum. I'm warning you now - if you don't make your own, you'll find yourself drunkenly calling friends and begging them to bring you a brick of refrigerated cookie dough for the love of all that's holy. Anyone raised in North America is incapable of smelling butter, vanilla and brown sugar without craving cookie dough. This is a scientifically proven fact.

So, now that you have your cookie dough going, it's time to get on with the boozy goodness. Add your brown sugar, vanilla, and butter to a bowl and cream it (that's blending it with a hand mixer for your non-cooks) until you have to fight the urge to add flour. Be strong. Instead, you're going to add the cinnamon, nutmeg, and allspice. At this point, you can put the mix into an airtight container and store it for up to a month.

When you're ready to serve, heat a teakettle full of water. Add 2 heaping tbsp of the butter batter and 2 shots of rum to a mug. Top it off with the boiling water and stir with a cinnamon stick. It'll taste fantastic with your fresh, hot cookies.

Martha Washington's Rum Punch

1 cup White Rum
1 cup Dark Rum
1 cup Orange Curacao
10 Lemons
8 Oranges
1/2 tsp Grated Nutmeg
6 Cloves
3 Cinnamon Sticks
10 cups Water
4 cups Sugar

Martha Washington preceded the Industrial Revolution by a generous score of years, but her Rum Punch was enjoyed in respectable homes across America for a good century after she passed on.

Bring the water to a boil and add the sugar. Stir well until the sugar is dissolved. Break the cinnamon sticks into small pieces and bruise the cloves in order to release their flavor then add them to the sugar water. Throw in the grated nutmeg while you're at it. Boil everything for 15 minutes, stirring occasionally.

Meanwhile, quarter all your lemons and six of your oranges. Add them to a large container and mash them. Not to disparage Martha as an ignorant colonial, but you could alternately add the juice, pulp and rind, leaving out the bitter white interior. Maybe she liked that bitter tang. Only drunken time traveling cultural anthropologists can know for sure.

Either way, get your citrus in a bowl and add your boiling sugar spice mix. Give it a good stir and let that mingle for a couple hours while it cools.

Once it reaches room temperature, strain away all the solids and add the booze. Slice your remaining two oranges into decorative wheels and float them on top of the punch. Serve iced, with an optional sprinkle of additional cinnamon and nutmeg.

WHISKEY COCKTAILS

Whiskey cocktails are split into two camps. In one we find the manly drinks of yesteryear when gentleman's clubs didn't permit ladies past the lobby and bitters were known to put hair on your chest. In the other, we find fruity, sweet farmhouse concoctions designed to kill the nasty flavor of less refined whiskey without diluting the alcohol content.

While the manliest of men may have pretended their testicles would ascend back into their bodies if they drank something made with more fruit than a fresh pie, the refined gentleman's cordial was really nothing more than an old fashioned farmhouse bounce with a bit of polish and some good marketing.

A whiskey bounce makes a lovely Steampunk drink. It marries authentic Victorian flavors to Industrial Era efficiency with a saucy mistress of surprisingly useful alcoholic fruit on the side. If you're in the mood for an impressive spread, you can always make either a chutney or glacee ice from the leftover fruit.

For Colonials, the classic bounce recipe comes from Martha Washington. Hers was made and emulated for so long that in 1913, a prohibition minded preacher in Edith Warton's *The Custom of the Country* rewrote the legend of George Washington chopping down the cherry tree so that the first president's secret motivations were to prevent the production of that devil drink Cherry Bounce. This was ironic since he would cheerfully take entire barrels of Martha's Cherry Bounce with him on long voyages.

People were still making Martha's recipe well into the First World War. For confused time travelers or those Steampunks who dabble in multiple eras of recreation, this drink will suit you well at any point over a good 200 year span. You can still follow Martha's directions to the letter.

"Extract the Juice of 20 pounds of well ripend Morrella Cherrys. Add to this 10 quarts of Old French brandy and sweeten it with White Sugar to your taste—To 5 Gallons of this mixture add one ounce of Spice Such as Cinnamon, Cloves and Nutmegs of each an Equal quantity Slightly bruis'd and a pint and half of Cherry kernels that have been gently broken in a mortar—After the liquor has fermented let it Stand Close-Stoped for a month or Six weeks—then bottle it remembering to put a lump of Loaf Sugar into each bottle."

You'll find recipes for less industrial quantities of bounces and cordials below, followed by a few of the whiskey cocktails which started gaining popularity in the late 19th century.

Cheating Cherry Bounce

2 pounds of frozen Cherries
2 cups Water
2 cups Sugar
1 bottle Whiskey
1 Cinnamon Stick

Dump your cherries into a large saucepan and add two cups of water. Simmer the cherries for about 15 minutes, mashing them gently to release the flavor. You don't need to bring them to a boil, although you won't ruin anything if you accidentally let them heat up too much. Add the sugar and cinnamon stick and stir well until the sugar is fully dissolved. Let it simmer for another 15 minutes, continuing to stir and mash the cherries. If you like spiced drinks, feel free to also add half a dozen cloves or some nutmeg.

Let the cherry mix cool to room temperature, then pour it and your bottle of whiskey into a sizeable nonreactive container, such as a large glass mason jar. Give it a good shake then leave it for anywhere from 3 weeks to 6 months. The longer you leave it alone, the more mellow your flavor.

When you're ready to drink it, strain your cherry bounce through cheesecloth before serving. It'll stay good in the fridge for a few days. If you're at risk of not drinking the whole batch, you can also bottle it.

The difference between this and the recipe for making cherry cordial liqueur (a staple of many early 20th century cocktails) is to simply substitute vodka for the whiskey. You have now doubled both the price and perceived class of your product.

Whatever you call your concoction, you now have a tasty drink and a big pile of alcoholic fruit. The cherries lost most of their structure by marinating in whiskey for half a year, but they'll still have plenty of flavor and a little bit of texture. You can go the simple route and just use them as an ice cream topping, but that's far from your only option. Remove the cinnamon stick and any other spices then throw the cherries into a food processor. You can now mix the tasty paste into your chutneys to add a bit of boozy zing or use them to make alcoholic cherry ice.

Cherry Bounce Ice

Leftover cherries from making Cherry Bounce
1 cup Sugar
4 cups Water
1 tsp ground Cinnamon

Bring the water to a boil. Add the cinnamon and sugar and stir well until it's dissolved. Put your leftover cherry bounce fruit into a food processor and blend until it's little more than paste. Add it to the sugar water and mix until well blended.

Pour the result into a wide, shallow, freezer-proof container and put it in the freezer until it becomes a solid. Every hour or so loosen it up with the tines of a fork. You want a nice, icy slush, not ice cubes. Once it reaches your desired consistency, rough it up with the fork once more and serve as a dessert. Once roughened up to give it texture, you can store it in the freezer for however long you'd like.

Easy Cherry Bounce

2 gallons Whiskey
1/2 gallon Cherry Juice
1 pound Sugar
4 Cinnamon Sticks
6 Cloves

If you can find bottled cherry juice you'll save yourself a lot of hassle and a few days of odd fingernail coloring. If you can't, you'll have to juice your own. As a consolation prize, you'll have all those useful cherry pits left over.

Mix the pound of sugar into your two gallons of whiskey until it's no longer visibly grainy. Now add everything else. If you juiced your own cherries, take 1 cup of the pits and crush them beneath your mighty canned goods. They add an interesting depth of flavor the juice alone lacks.

If you're feeling extra lazy, you can throw four pounds of fresh Cherries into a food processor, pits and all. You're going to strain out all the solids in a few months anyway. Let the blade roughen up your pits and turn your cherries into paste.

Regardless of how you acquired your cherries, at this point, everything should be hanging out in a single airtight container. Seal it up so the flavors can spend some quality time getting to know one another. Six months is enough for them to form a good, solid relationship, but the longer you let it sit the mellower the flavor.

When you're ready to drink it, strain the Cherry Bounce through cheesecloth to remove any solids and pour it into a decanter. It'll stay drinkable in the fridge for 3-4 days, or you can bottle it and enjoy at your leisure.

Ginger Cordial

1 gallon Whiskey
1 gallon Water
10 cups White Sugar
10 Lemons
6 inches fresh, raw Ginger Root

Peel the ginger and mince it finely. Dice your 10 lemons. Yes, really. Dice them. Mix the diced lemons and minced ginger with the whiskey and seal it up tight. Wash your hands and give yourself about 3 weeks to forget what you just did.

Open the container. Stare in perplexed confusion at the diced lemons, then vow to just get on with it. Maybe the bitter white interior of the lemons added an interesting flavor note. Pretend you believe that.

Boil your water and dissolve the sugar in it. Once you have a nice simple syrup, let it cool to room temperature. Strain the whiskey through cheesecloth to remove the lemon and ginger pieces. Mix the simple syrup and strained whiskey in an airtight container and leave it the heck alone for at least 3 months, preferably closer to six.

Meanwhile, mix the ginger lemons with 2 cups of ice. Slowly force them into the hungry maw of your garbage disposal. You'll give it a refreshing lemony scent while the acids clean away some of the collected gunk.

Peach Cordial

5 pounds frozen Peaches
1 gallon Whiskey
1 pound Sugar
1 Cinnamon Stick (optional)

The original recipe started with a peck of peaches and 5 gallons of whiskey. That's a lot of cordial. If you live in a peach growing area and want to make this fresh, feel free to acquire around 7 pounds of soft peaches late in the season. Cut them into slices and save about two cups of the stones. Otherwise, just buy the frozen peach slices.

Mix the sugar into the whiskey until it's pretty much dissolved. Add the peaches (including two cups of broken, bruised stones, if you opted for fresh fruit) and give it a good stir. You can add a nicely bruised cinnamon stick for a hint of additional flavor. Just like the rest of the cordial recipes, put everything in a nice airtight container and leave it alone for 3-6 months. When you come back, strain out the solids, drink the liquids, and bottle anything you don't chug.

If you enjoy recipes with peach schnapps, this is a great homemade substitute. A shot also adds a delightful flavor to iced tea.

Raspberry Cordial

4 gallons Whiskey
4 quarts Raspberries
4 pounds Sugar

This is a good use for dubious raspberries on your grocery store's produce clearance shelf. It doesn't matter if they have a little mold on them or if they've all gone mushy. You're going to mash them into a paste anyway.

If it's not raspberry season, buy four pounds of frozen berries. Put them in a bowl and let them thaw until they're room temperature, retaining all the precious juice.

Whether you have moldy old berries or recently defrosted ones, mash the heck out of them until the interior of your bowl resembles the after effects of a zombie attack. Mix in the sugar. Cover the dubiously pulpy mess and let it sit at room temperature for at least 24 hours.

When you come back, it'll appear that your zombie bite has bled out horribly in the bowl. Strain everything through cheesecloth. Really squeeze the last bits of juice out of the cheesecloth until your sugar is as dry as a desiccated corpse.

Now add the whiskey, give it a nice stir, and leave it in a cool, dark place for a week. That's right - a week. Sure, you can leave it to mellow for months, but this is allegedly quite drinkable in a fraction the time.

If you're in the mood for a once in a lifetime period drink, substitute white vinegar for the whiskey. Yes, really. Few people today voluntarily try the vinegar version of this cordial twice, but it was once popular over ice. Try not to think too hard about that. You'll lose sleep.

Currant Cordial

1 gallon Whiskey
1 pound Currants
1 pound Sugar
1 inch peeled Ginger
Rind of 2 Lemons

Currants used to be an incredibly popular fruit in the United States. However, at the turn of the 20th century it was discovered currant shrubs hosted a disease called white pine blister rot fungus. As you can guess from the name, it was devastating for pine trees. The US Federal government banned cultivation in order to protect tree farms. The ban was lifted in 1966, but it has taken quite awhile for a few local farmers to try planting the shrubs again.

If you can find fresh or frozen currants in your part of the country (or you're in the United Kingdom), take advantage of the opportunity to taste some real history. You won't find anything in a liquor store matching the flavor.

Gently mash the currants in a large, non-reactive container (glass or crockery are preferred). Dice the peeled ginger. Throw that in there along with the lemon rind and whiskey. Give the whole mess a good stir, then cover it up and let it sit for 24 hours.

The next day, strain all your liquids through some cheesecloth. Add the pound of sugar to the liquids and stir until it's as blended as possible. If you're so inclined, you can throw the solids into a food processor and make an alcoholic currant paste which goes nicely in chutneys, glacees, or ice creams.

After twelve hours have passed, give your sugary mess one more stir. You can allegedly drink it now, though everyone agrees it'll be better if you let it sit for at least three months.

Hot Whiskey

6 shots hot Water
2 shots Whiskey
1 tsp Sugar
1 thick cut Lemon Wedge
1 Cinnamon Stick
Nutmeg

Boil some water as though you're going to make a mug of tea. At this point you can either remember you're in the mood for a tasty adult beverage or pretend you lost the teabags. Either way, you can't let this freshly boiled water go to waste.

Fill a mug with the whiskey, sugar and water. Squeeze your lemon wedge into the mix and stir it all with a lightly bruised cinnamon stick. Let the cinnamon stick soak in the mug while you wait for it to cool enough to drink. Sprinkle a dash of nutmeg on top and enjoy. This may not literally put hair on your chest, but it'll certainly keep you warm on a winter night.

Bitsy Highball

1 shot Whiskey
1 shot Sherry
1 shot Pineapple Juice
Juice of 1/2 Lemon

It's time to get out your cocktail shaker! Fill that bad boy half way with ice then dump in all of your ingredients. Shake it like you're stuck in a fast paced game of whack-a-mole. Pour the entire contents of the shaker, ice and all, into a highball glass. Garnish it with a wedge cut from your remaining half a lemon. One of these a day will keep the scurvy at bay.

Old Fashioned

2 shots Whiskey (preferably Bourbon)
1 thick cut Orange Wedge
2 Maraschino Cherries
2 dashes Bitters
1 tsp Sugar

This is called an Old Fashioned because by the time people got around to writing cocktail books this was already a grandpa drink. Instead of asking for it by name, people would tell the bartender not to make any newfangled nonsense. Just give them an old fashioned cocktail. The name stuck.

It's a wonderfully simple, classic drink that heartily deserves its two centuries of popularity. To make it, drop your orange wedge, cherries, sugar, and bitters into the bottom of a lowball glass. Muddle them together until the orange looks thoroughly abused. Leave the fruit in place. Add the whiskey, give it all a good stir, and fill the rest of the glass with ice.

Undeserving girly men or children under the age of 9 may add a couple shots of water to dilute the majesty before topping the glass with ice.

Manhattan

1 shot Whiskey
1/2 shot Sweet Vermouth
1/2 shot Dry Vermouth
1 dash Bitters
Twist of Lemon or a Cherry

This is another classic late 19th century cocktail. People have argued about how to make the perfect Manhattan for over a century. This recipe merely claims to be effective, not sublime.

Add all the ingredients to a cocktail shaker along with half a dozen ice cubes. Give it a hearty, enthusiastic shake, then strain the result into a martini glass. Garnish it with a twist of lemon or a cherry. If you're feeling extra daring, you could even garnish it with an olive.

No matter how you make your Manhattan, be prepared for cocktail geeks to passionately argue that everything you do is wrong. Have fun letting them mix one "the right way" in opposition to your meager offering, then ask well corseted ladies to volunteer for a taste test. Let the cocktail snob win the battle and mix your new lady friend a different drink.

Bloody Brandy

1 shot Whiskey
1 shot Cherry Brandy
1/2 shot Sweet Vermouth
Juice of 1/2 Blood Orange
1 tsp Sugar
1 dash Orange Bitters

Blood oranges are popular among cooks and Klingons, but everyone else tends to find them unnecessarily bitter. This is a much better drink when made with a regular orange, but sadly looks far less dramatic in the glass.

Dump everything into a cocktail shaker and fill it about halfway with ice. Shake like you're trying to restore circulation to a numb limb. Strain the result into a martini glass. Admire the color then garnish it with a wedge cut from the other half of your blood orange. This is a great drink to carry when you're trying to pace yourself. You'll never want more than a sip.

GIN COCKTAILS

Contrary to popular belief, a Gin and Tonic a day will not keep malaria away. You need around 300 mg of quinine taken three times a day for effective treatment. Modern tonic water has around 20 mg. While British soldiers in India did sweeten their quinine with lemon and sugar to make it more palatable, they'd already been throwing back every variation of gin drink they could get their hands on for the last hundred years.

The thing that really set gin apart in the 19th century was the sheer anti-social nature of gin recipes. You don't make ten gallons of gin punch to serve at a party. You throw some gin and a few more palatable ingredients into a cocktail shaker then go sit in a dark corner and enjoy your own personal beverage.

Most of these drinks lack the spirit of adventure found in less depressing 19th century drinks. Instead of leaving dubious dairy products to sit out at room temperature for two days or risking your life with raw eggs, you merely dump a few things into a cocktail shaker if they're uncarbonated or a highball glass if they have some fizz. Gin drinks are certainly faster to prepare and arguably less likely to end in medical trauma, but they lack that bold sensation that the devil may come tomorrow, so best live it up today.

Think of Gin cocktails as the fast food of the Steampunk world - something to be prepared quickly and consumed alone.

Victorian Lemonade

2 shots Gin
2 shots Water
1 tsp Sugar
Juice of 1/2 Lemon
Mint Leaves

Squeeze half your lemon into the bottom of an empty cocktail shaker. Add a few mint leaves (2-4 based on personal taste) and muddle the mint in the juice. Don't worry if you've never muddled before. You're an adult. It's a perfectly natural behavior, and quite a few people enjoy it immensely. I promise, it won't even put hair on your palms.

To muddle, merely use something blunt, such as a pestle, to bruise the heck out of the leaves so they release all their minty goodness.

Now add the rest of your ingredients along with a handful of ice. Shake like you're imagining what lies above a lady's ankles. Once you've finished working up a sweat, pour the drink into an iced lowball glass and garnish it with a wedge cut from the other half of your lemon.

Ginger Gin

6 shots Ginger Beer
2 shots Gin
3-4 dashes Bitters

Mix everything in a highball glass and give it a good stir. Top the glass off with ice and garnish it with a lime wedge.

You can pretend this drink exists to aid in digesting a hearty platter of fish and chips, but really, the ginger exists to hide the flavor of the gin so you won't notice how drunk you are when those friendly men in the corner mug you later tonight.

Teaplanter Cocktail

6 shots Lemonade
1 shot Gin
2 dashes Bitters
Orange Wedge
1 Maraschino Cherry

Despite the name this drink contains neither tea nor potting soil.

Mix the lemonade, gin, and bitters in a highball glass. Give it a good stir, fill the glass with ice, then squeeze the orange wedge over the top. Garnish with a cherry.

English Rose

1 1/2 shots Gin
1 shot Apricot Brandy
1/2 shot Dry Vermouth
1 tsp Grenadine Syrup
2 thick Lemon Wedges
1 Cherry

Dump your gin, brandy, vermouth, grenadine, and the juice from one thick lemon wedge into a cocktail shaker and fill it about halfway with ice. Give it a nice aggressive shake, then strain your cocktail into an iced lowball glass. Squeeze the remaining lemon wedge over the top and garnish it with a cherry.

If you think three shots might be excessive for a single drink, strain the cocktail into two martini glasses instead, top both with a hearty squeeze of lemon, and share the fruits of your labor with a friend.

Gimlet

1 shot Gin
1/2 shot Simple Syrup
Juice of 1/2 Lime
Lime Wedge

This simple, classic cocktail has scared countless people away from gin. It's vitally important that you don't shop the bottom of the shelf when making a Gimlet. If you're spending less than $30 on a bottle of gin, you might as well use Pine-Sol instead.

To make a Gimlet, simply add your gin, lime juice and simple syrup (or, if you're feeling lazy, 1 tsp of sugar) to an icy cocktail shaker and shake it for a mere 5-10 seconds. Strain the result into a chilled Martini glass and garnish it with a wedge of lime.

Inhale that pungent pine aroma. A bad Gimlet tastes like drinking the tears of a homeless orphan crying against a Christmas tree. No one is entirely sure what a good gimlet tastes like.

Orange Abby

2 shots Gin
2 shots Orange Juice
2 dashes Orange Bitters
Long Stemmed Cherry

The flavors of orange and (good, expensive) gin blend surprisingly well with a couple dashes of bitters. Put everything but the cherry into an icy cocktail shaker and shake it like you're a mobster coaxing poorbox money out of a priest. Strain the result into a martini glass and garnish it with a cherry.

Dry Orange

2 shots Gin
1 shot Orange Juice
1/2 shot Dry Vermouth
1/2 shot Sweet Vermouth
Orange Wedge

Put everything but your orange wedge into a cocktail shaker half full of ice. Shake it for 15-30 seconds, strain it into a martini glass, and garnish it with a thick wedge of orange.

Gin Kirsch Cocktail

2 shots Gin
1 shot Kirsch
1 shot Apricot Brandy
1/2 shot Lemon Juice
1 tsp Sugar
Lemon Rind Twist

By this point I'm sure you will be shocked to learn everything but the lemon rind goes into an icy cocktail shaker. Whenever you think you're done shaking, keep going for another 5-10 seconds in order to really blend the sugar. Pour the result into a lowball glass, fill it with ice, and garnish it with a twist of lemon rind.

If you don't like the taste of gin, it's worth substituting vodka just to enjoy the blend of Kirsch and Apricot Brandy, both fine ingredients which have sadly gone out of fashion.

Merry Widow

2 shots Gin
1 shot Dry Vermouth
1 tsp Pernod
1 tsp Benedictine
2 dashes Orange Bitters
Lemon Wedge

Pernod and Benedictine are both very strong, distinctive flavors which I personally do not believe play nicely together. However, the Victorians loved pitting strong, opposing flavors together in a sort of culinary death match to be fought on the battlefield of your tongue. If you enjoy this drink, you were truly born in the wrong era.

Once more, everything but the Lemon wedge garnish goes into a well iced cocktail shaker to be pounded like mustachioed gentlemen in a back alley cage match. Once the opposing forces within are plenty angry from being shaken about, unceremoniously dump them into the battlefield of a lowball glass. Lightly squeeze your lemon on top then mount it on the edge of the glass as a garnish.

Anyone who believes everyday life was better in the Victorian era should be forced to try this drink once.

Sloe Gin Fizz

2 shots Sloe Gin
Juice of 1/2 Lemon
1 tsp Sugar
1 Egg White
1 dash Bitters
Tonic Water
Orange Slice or Cherry

Sloe Gin is a bright red gin based liqueur made with sloe berries and not, as some people believe, gin distilled from the blood of sloths. It seems every other generation alternately loves or hates it.

Add your Sloe Gin, the juice of 1/2 lemon, sugar, egg white, and bitters to an ice filled cocktail shaker. You want the egg white nice and frothy, so keep shaking for another 5-10 seconds after you think you should be done.

Strain the result into a highball glass half full of ice. Top it off with tonic water and give it a gentle stir with a straw. Garnish the drink with an orange wedge or a cherry.

Gin Milk

2 shots Gin
1 cup Milk
1 tsp Sugar
Nutmeg

This is a pretty straightforward drink. Sometimes, you want to enjoy a nice glass of milk, but you also want to be drunk. Luckily, you can do both at the same time by adding your gin, milk, and sugar to a cocktail shaker and beating it about with some ice. Pour the whole shaker - ice, milk mix, and all - into a highball glass and top it off with a nice dusting of nutmeg. Spice makes it nutritious, right?

Fallen Angel

2 shots Gin
1 tsp Creme de Methe
Juice of 1/2 Lime
2 dashes Bitters

This is one of my favorite examples of a drink where none of the ingredients belong together. To add an extra air of improbability, throw in a shot of heavy cream.

Whether or not you use the heavy cream, dump everything into a cocktail shaker with a scant handful of ice. Shake hard and try not to contemplate what you're about to drink. Pour the entire contents of the shaker, ice and all, into a lowball glass and get ready for one of the most interesting things that can happen to your mouth.

Fogcutter

1 shot Gin
1/2 shot White Rum
1/2 shot Brandy
1/2 shot Cherry Brandy
1 tsp Sugar
2 dashes Orange Bitters

Throw your gin, white rum, brandy, sugar and orange bitters into a cocktail shaker. Fill the shaker about halfway with ice and show the ingredients a good time, granted you think being bounced about in a narrow metal tube is fun.

Once it's sufficiently abused, strain the resulting mix into a round champagne glass. Float the cherry brandy on top and attempt to set it on fire. If you succeed, bask in applause and admiration from the ladies. If you fail, shrug it off and throw the drink back as though it's a shot.

Cool Gin Cucumber

2 shots Gin
4 inches English Cucumber, seeded
1 tsp Simple Syrup
2-4 Mint Leaves

This is my personal favorite gin drink. It's light, refreshing, and its availability is the minimum standard by which I judge bars.

Cut your cucumber in half and strip out the seeds. Chop the cucumber into a few more pieces before dropping it in the bottom of a cocktail shaker. Aggressively muddle the heck out of the cucumber until it's little more than paste. You want the precious juices. Add in the mint leaves and keep muddling. You can't pummel it enough. Trust me, I've tried. The more aggressive you get, the better it tastes.

Once your arm is tired, add in the gin and simple syrup (or, if you're lazy, 2 tsp of straight sugar), fill the shaker halfway with ice and hand it to someone who isn't already tired from all that muddling. Once you've amused yourself watching them pound your drink, have them strain it into a martini glass. Garnish with a thick slice of cucumber, sit back, and enjoy the refreshing goodness.

If you want a slightly more savory taste, some people swear by a dash of either straight or orange bitters.

ABSINTHE COCKTAILS

Nineteenth century drinkers knew something we seem to have forgotten. A little Absinthe goes a long way. Sure, libertines like Byron would chug entire bottles, but he also knowingly shagged his half-sister. Reasonable people enjoyed the idea that Absinthe let them flirt with danger while also understanding the reality that it tastes like melted licorice stored in gym socks. The kind of people who really like the flavor of Absinthe also do straight shots of Ouzo.

Go ahead and buy a $50 bottle of imported Absinthe to take to a convention. If you play your cards right, you'll use less than a quarter of it while creating an air of generosity and mystique. If you use these recipes, you'll probably also be the only person at the convention to make a drinkable Absinthe cocktail.

Egg in a Blanket

1/2 shot Absinthe
1 shot Brandy
1 large Egg White
1 tsp Sugar
1 dash Orange Bitters
Lime Slice

Toss everything into a cocktail shaker. Fill it half way with ice and shake with the fury of a moderately sized waterfall. Strain the contents into a white wine glass and garnish with a slice of lime.

Creamy Green Violets

1 shot Gin
1 shot Heavy Cream
1 tsp Sweet Vermouth
1 tsp Violet Water
1 tsp Absinthe
1 tsp Sugar

You make violet water by plucking the petals off violets and soaking them in water for anywhere from 1 to 4 days. Strain out the solids, refrigerate the liquids, and enjoy an exotic period ingredient. The same technique works equally well for rosemary or lavender, other flavors enjoyed in Victorian cocktails.

Don't fall prey to the temptation to use a shot of Absinthe instead of a teaspoon. Let it flavor the drink without overpowering it.

Add all your ingredients to a cocktail shaker along with a scant handful of ice. Spend a minute giving it a good, enthusiastic shake before straining the contents into a martini glass. If available, garnish with a violet petal.

Ballantine

1/2 shot Gin
1/2 shot Sweet Vermouth
1 tsp Absinthe
2 dashes Orange Bitters

Put away the cocktail shaker. Instead, add everything to a brandy snifter and swish it gently. This cocktail smells better than it tastes, making it perfect for anyone seeking an excuse to nurse a drink all night.

Blackthorn Cocktail

1 shot Irish Whiskey
1/2 shot Vermouth
1 tsp Absinthe
3 dashes Bitters

Arguably, this cocktail could use more sugar and less vermouth. It's a manly, bitter drink designed for people who have lost all sense of joy in life.

Add everything to a lowball glass and stir gently. Top with ice and garnish with tears.

Green Brazilian

1/2 shot Sherry
1/2 shot Sweet Vermouth
1/2 shot Absinthe
1 dash Bitters
1 tsp Sugar
Lemon Wedge

Absolutely nothing about this comes from Brazil. One can't help but wonder if a Brazilian bartender somewhere in 1880's Manhattan made it as a parody of popular British drinks. The truth is lost to time, but sadly the recipe remains.

Fill a cocktail shaker with your sherry, vermouth, absinthe, sugar, bitters and despair. Add in a few ice cubes and give it a lackluster, unenthusiastic shaking as you contemplate your own mortality. Rather than strain it, just dump everything, ice and all, into a lowball glass. Since it doesn't look bitter enough, squeeze your lemon wedge on top. Drink with the resignation that life didn't work out the way you hoped.

Little Egypt

2 shots Scotch Whiskey
2 shots Sherry
1 tsp Absinthe
2 dashes Bitters
1 dash Vermouth
Slice of Lime

This entirely reasonable quantity of Absinthe should join all its other friends in a lowball glass. Gently stir them together to encourage the flavors to mingle, then throw in some ice cubes for them to play on. Garnish with a slice of lime, which will enviously watch the party from the rim of your glass, always wondering why no one likes it.

Morning Daisy

2 shots Scotch Whiskey
1 Egg White
1 tsp Absinthe
1 tsp Sugar
1 tsp Lemon Juice
Twist of Lemon

Add everything but the lemon twist to a cocktail shaker then fill it about halfway up with ice. Shake like you're trying to punch an invisible alarm clock that won't stop buzzing. Pour the result into a martini glass and garnish it with a twist of lemon.

Saratoga Brace Up

1 Egg
1 shot Brandy
1 tsp Absinthe
1 tsp Sugar
2 dashes Bitters
Juice of one thick Lemon wedge
Juice of one thick Lime wedge
Tonic Water
Long Stemmed Cherry

Put everything but the tonic water into a cocktail shaker then add ice until the shaker is about half full. Shake with the vigor of a celibate vicar. Strain the foamy white result into a highball glass. Top the glass off with tonic water and stir gently. Garnish the result with a long stemmed cherry.

Horse Thief Cocktail

1 shot Gin
1/2 shot Vermouth
1/4 shot Absinthe

The simplicity of this drink does nothing to make up for its taste. Add everything to a martini glass, give it a gentle stir, and serve at room temperature. with a lukewarm apology.

Green Russian

2 shots Heavy Cream
1 shot Vodka
1 shot Absinthe
1 tsp Sugar
Mint Leaf

Vodka wasn't unknown in the 19th century, but in Western Europe and the Americas, it wasn't terribly popular. This probably has a lot to do with the fact that most vodka at that time was about as smooth as bathtub gin and about half as safe. The mystique no doubt added to the appeal of this drink.

Add everything but the mint leaf to a lowball glass and stir gently. Top the glass off with ice and garnish it with the mint leaf. If you're not a fan of bitter, milky licorice, feel free to reduce the Absinthe to a more reasonable single teaspoon rather than a single shot.

82296393R10095

Made in the USA
Columbia, SC
30 November 2017